THE PREDICAMENT OF HOMECOMING
Cultural and Social Life of
North African Immigrants in Israel

SYMBOL, MYTH, AND RITUAL

Series Editor: Victor Turner

Shlomo Deshen and Moshe Shokeid, *The Predicament of Homecoming: Cultural and Social Life of North African Immigrants in Israel*

Frederick K. Errington, *Karavar: Masks and Power in a Melanesian Ritual*

Barbara G. Myerhoff, *Peyote Hunt: The Sacred Journey of the Huichol Indians*

Victor Turner, *Dramas, Fields, and Metaphors: Symbolic Action in Human Society*

Frank E. Manning, *Black Clubs in Bermuda: Ethnography of a Play World*

Raymond Firth, *Symbols: Public and Private*

Nancy D. Munn, *Walbiri Iconography: Graphic Representation and Cultural Symbolism in a Central Australian Society*

Mircea Eliade, *Australian Religions: An Introduction*

THE PREDICAMENT
OF HOMECOMING

Cultural and Social Life of
North African Immigrants
in Israel

SHLOMO DESHEN and
MOSHE SHOKEID

Cornell University Press

ITHACA AND LONDON

First published 1974 by Cornell University Press.
Published in the United Kingdom by Cornell University Press Ltd., 2-4 Brook Street, London W1Y 1AA.

International Standard Book Number 0-8014-0885-7
Library of Congress Catalog Card Number 74-4902

Printed in the United States of America by Vail-Ballou Press, Inc.

To those who came from
the Atlas Mountains, Djerba,
Gabès, and elsewhere

Foreword

Recently both the research and theoretical concerns of many anthropologists have once again been directed toward the role of symbols—religious, mythic, aesthetic, political, and even economic—in social and cultural processes. Whether this revival is a belated response to developments in other disciplines (psychology, ethology, philosophy, linguistics, to name only a few), or whether it reflects a return to a central concern after a period of neglect, is difficult to say. In recent field studies, anthropologists have been collecting myths and rituals in the context of social action, and improvements in anthropological field technique have produced data that are richer and more refined than heretofore; these new data have probably challenged theoreticians to provide more adequate explanatory frames. Whatever may have been the causes, there is no denying a renewed curiosity about the nature of the connections between culture, cognition, and perception, as these connections are revealed in symbolic forms.

Although excellent individual monographs and articles in symbolic anthropology or comparative symbology have recently appeared, a common focus or forum that can be provided by a topically organized series of books has not been available. The present series is intended to fill this lacuna. It is designed to include not only field monographs and theoretical and comparative studies by anthropologists, but also work by scholars in other disciplines, both scientific and humanistic. The appearance of studies in such a forum encourages emulation, and emulation can produce fruitful new theories. It is therefore our hope that the series will serve as a house of many mansions, providing hospitality for the practitioners of any discipline that has a serious and creative concern with comparative symbology. Too often, disciplines are sealed off, in sterile pedantry, from significant intellectual influences. Nevertheless, our primary aim is to bring to public attention works on ritual and myth written by anthropologists, and our readers will find a variety of strictly anthropological approaches ranging from formal analyses of systems of symbols to empathetic accounts of divinatory and initiatory rituals.

VICTOR TURNER

University of Chicago

Contents

Illustrations

PLATES

FIGURES

Preface

S. N. EISENSTADT

Recently sociologists and anthropologists have stressed the importance of relating studies of the autonomy of a society's symbols with studies of its social organizations. This book applies, in an interesting way, this and other new emphases to the study of immigrants in general and several "oriental" Jewish communities in particular.

The studies of absorption of immigrants in Israel undertaken over the last twenty years have been varied. Early research analyzed broad structural and demographic trends and the general characteristics of the process of absorption (see Eisenstadt 1953); later works dealt with the integration of different groups of immigrants into the emerging social structure and their impact upon it. The examination of processes of absorption in the agricultural settlements—especially in cooperative *moshavim*—has been among the most important of this later work. In some studies (for example, Willner 1969), the analysis of the policy and process of absorption of immigrants in such settlements has served as a starting point for an analysis of the general process of nation-building in Israel. The Department of Sociology in the Hebrew University and the Department of Rural Settlement of the Jewish Agency, in a cooperative venture, have conducted further studies. Some of these focused on the comparison of cooperative *moshavim* with other types of rural settlements. The work of Weintraub, Lissak, and Atzmon (1969) is an example. Weintraub and his collaborators later (1971) conducted intensive comparative studies of different immigrant groups within these settlements. Weingrod (1966) and the rural sociologists attached to the Department of Rural Settlement of the Jewish Agency (especially Shapiro 1971) carried out a series of case studies of different settlements and of different aspects of their dynamics—studies, for example, of how relationships between generations adjusted to different types of technology.

This work emphasized above all the process of change among the groups of traditional immigrants as they settled in the *moshavim*—the dynamics of their transformation from peasants, peddlers, or urban members of traditional minority communities into modern farmers and into citizens of Israel and, within the traditional setting of these groups, the factors that influence the different degrees of success of this process of transformation, or its breakdown. These factors include cultural orientation, family cohesion, leadership structure, and the like.

These studies strongly stress the relations between organizations at the microstructure of the settlement and at the macrostructure of Israeli society. Similar emphases also characterize several social studies undertaken under the auspices of the Department of Social Anthropology of the University of Manchester, under the supervision of Max Gluckman, in which Shlomo Deshen and Moshe Shokeid participated and which studied much more intensively the structural dynamics of various smaller units—whether *moshavim* or urban quarters (see Baldwin 1972, Deshen 1970, Shokeid 1971b).

Thus most of these studies—whether stemming from sociological or social anthropological tradition—evinced very strong structural-organizational orientations; cultural factors were mostly seen within the framework of such organizational settings, influencing these new settlements or adapting themselves to them.

The present work, while strongly rooted in this tradition, and while providing many important new insights into the dynamics of these processes, adds a new dimension to the study of the absorption of immigrants in Israel. This dimension is related to those new developments in sociological, especially anthropological, theory that emphasize the autonomy of the symbolic spheres. In its most extreme form this stance has been connected with the work of Lévi-Strauss. But if Lévi-Strauss in his latest work has neglected problems of social organization, other anthropologists and sociologists—such as Geertz (1960), Turner (1967), Beidelman (1972), Tiryakian (1970), and Dumont (1970) in his studies of Indian civilization—have stressed the importance of combining this new work on the autonomy of the symbolic sphere with studies of social organization. This growing concern with the symbolic dimension of social life and the stress on its autonomy was paralleled by a shift in the theoretical assumptions in one area of studies of social change (to which many of the studies in Israel were closely connected), namely the study of modernization.

Perhaps the central motive for the shift has been dissatisfaction with the theory that supposed a total dichotomy between traditional and modern societies and that assumed that the destruction of traditional forms of life is necessary for successful modernization. There has been a growing recognition that traditional forms do more than merely "persist" in, or influence the degree to which different groups adjust to, new, modern settings. Instead, it is increasingly recognized that these forces may also shape or influence the contours of the emerging modern settings. Indeed, these contours may evince a high degree of continuity with some of the institutional contours that prevailed in these societies in their "traditional" settings (see in greater detail Eisenstadt 1973a, b).

These considerations, including tensions and contradictions in the symbolic sphere itself, have pointed out the importance of relating changes in the symbolic sphere to changes in the structural-organizational system. We now have to consider the nature of this relation and of the institutional anchorage of these symbols.

This book provides very interesting contributions to the discussion of such problems. The authors focus not only on the structural-organizational changes and transformations that take place in different, mostly "traditional," immigrant groups in Israel, but also on the transformations of the symbolic dimensions of their life. These problems are discussed in the context of, and in relation to, concrete structural settings.

The studies of the transformation of the symbolic realm presented here are, broadly speaking, of two kinds— although no such rough classification can really do justice to the richness of the materials and analyses. One type is best illustrated by Chapters 7 and 8, which provide fascinating cases of the mechanisms of the crystallization and transformation of symbols of subcollective identity. These processes are of great interest in the context of a much broader problem—that of the nature of ethnic identity. The authors indicate that the very existence of such ethnic identity cannot be taken as "given." The basic identity of these groups in the past was that of Jew, not of "Moroccan" or "oriental." The situation of immigration and absorption in Israel has created their new, paradoxical identity which distinguishes them from other Jews. The other line of analysis, best illustrated in Chapters 2, 3, 4, 5, and 6, emphasizes the way the meaning of the various broader cultural and religious symbols is transformed for individuals, who search within their new environment for ways of reorganizing their cognitive structure and affective and social orientations.

Such processes of change impinge on existing patterns of social life and cultural traditions, undermining them and threatening social and psychological security. At the same time, they open up new social and cultural horizons, vistas of participation in new institutional and cultural orders. But the degree to which the existing patterns are undermined, as well as the scope and nature of the new vistas, naturally varies greatly in different situations, as do also the "reactions" to these changes and the ways that the elites and the other members of the society solve the concomitant problems.

In many situations of change, cultural traditions, symbols, artifacts, and organizations become more elaborate and articulated, more rationally organized, and more formalized, and different groups and individuals in a society acquire a greater awareness of them. Concomitantly tradition tends to become differentiated in layers. Simple "given" usages or patterns of behavior can become quite distinct from more articulate and formalized symbols of cultural order, such as great ritual centers and offices, theological codices, or special buildings. Each layer of tradition tends to vary also in the degree and nature of its prescriptive validity and in its relevance to particular spheres of social life (economic, administrative, or political). As most such social and cultural changes are usually connected with growing structural differentiation among these spheres, the spheres can be associated in different ways with both old and new traditions. To put it the other way round, the old and new traditions and symbols can be perceived as more or less relevant to these spheres in terms of prescribing the proper modes of behavior within them, in defining the goals prevalent in them, and in providing their overall "meaning."

Such processes are often related to a growing "partialization" and privatization of various traditions, especially of the older existing traditions. Even if the "old" customs and symbols are not negated, they undergo far-reaching changes. What has been the total sanctioned pattern of life of any given community, society, or individual tends to become only a partial one in several aspects. It can persist as binding only for some members of a society, or only in some spheres, and even the validity of its prescriptive power or of its use as the guiding symbolic template in these spheres of life can change greatly. Hence there always arise in such situations the problems, first, whether the old or the new traditions or symbols of traditions represent the true tradition of the new social, political, or religious community, and second, how far any given existing tradition can become incorporated into the new central patterns of culture and "tradition." In such situations, an uncertainty grows about the validity of the traditional (existing) sanctions for the new symbols and organizations, the scope and nature of the traditional sources of legitimacy of the new social, political, or cultural order, and the extent to which it is possible to legitimize this order in terms of the existing traditions.

In consequence, the several layers of tradition can differ in the degree to which they become foci of awareness and "problems" for different parts of the society. Sometimes in such situations the very traditionality of the given social and cultural order tends to be seen as a "problem," and this attitude or view might give rise to the erosion of any traditional commitment and to concomitant tendencies of social and cultural disorganization. People especially sensitive to such problems of symbolic templates may find that all these factors can seriously threaten their personal identity and its relation to the collective identity of their social and cultural orders. Both on the personal level and on the level of the more central symbols of tradition, there could arise, often as a reaction to the possibilities of erosion, the tendency known as traditionalism; there would then be a potential dichotomy between "tradition" and "traditionalism." Traditionalism is not to be confused with a "simple" or "natural" upkeep of a given tradition. It denotes an ideological mode and stance, a mode oriented against the new symbols, making some parts of the older tradition into the only legitimate symbols of the traditional order and upholding them to counter "new" trends. The "traditionalist" attitude tends thus toward formalization, on both the symbolic and the organizational levels.

When major institutions and traditions are undermined, the resulting possibilities of change open up and intensify— for those individuals, groups, or centers involved—the problems inherent in all situations. In more general terms, the individual, in such situations, tries to assure his basic social identity as a member of a society and as bearer of a cultural tradition. On the structural-organizational level, changing conditions challenge the ability of a society and its centers to organize new patterns of roles, groups, and institutional frameworks. On the cultural level, the society and its centers must develop symbols and traditions which give meaning to an individual's life and social activities, assure his personal and collective identities and the relations among them, and guide him in his choice of goals and patterns of social participation in changing circumstances.

More concretely, on the structural and organizational level, all groups or categories of people caught in situations of change must discover how to maintain or maximize their resources, how to retain or improve their absolute and/or relative power positions, how to maintain or improve their status, and how to compete with other groups in various institutional spheres. They all face the difficulty of developing the ability to participate, to some degree, in the new tasks, goals, and organizations which tend to develop in situations of change. But beyond this, groups or categories of people may face here a deeper problem—that of retaining or reformulating their identity in terms of their "pattern of life," their standing in the sociocultural order, and their relation to the center and to the basic referents and boundaries of the collective identity.

The processes of reconstitution of traditions may develop in several different dimensions, depending on the basic attitudes of the groups in the new situation. Several major patterns of reconstruction of tradition emerge in situations of social change in general, and of modernization in particular. The "traditionalistic" pattern segregates "traditional" (ritual, religious) and "nontraditional" spheres of life without, however, developing any appropriate symbolic and organizational bonds between the two. In other words, no new precepts or symbolic orientations develop that might serve as guides to the ways in which the various layers of tradition could become connected in meaningful patterns. At the same time, a strong predisposition or demand for some clear unifying principle tends to persist; uneasiness and insecurity become pronounced when this principle is lacking. As a result, a tendency can develop toward "ritualization" of the symbols of traditional life, on the personal and collective levels alike—a tendency closely related to the traditionalism discussed above. Increasing attempts to impose traditional symbols on the new secular world in a relatively rigid, militant way may then alternate with the total isolation of these traditional symbols from the impurities of that world. This response is often accompanied by an intolerance of ambiguity on both personal and collective levels, as well as by apathy and the erosion of any normative commitments because of such apathy. Social groups that exhibit such tendencies do not normally incorporate their various "primordial" symbols of local, ethnic caste, or class identity into the new center of the society, and the reformulation of these symbols on a new level of common identification is difficult and problematic. Rather, the symbols tend to become foci of separateness, of ritual traditionalism. On a macrosocietal level, these tendencies are usually characterized by conservative ideologies, coercive orientations and policies, and an active ideological or symbolic closure of the new center, with a strong traditionalistic emphasis on older symbols.

In an alternative process of reconstitution—an adaptive or transformative one—there is a continuous distinction and differentiation among the various layers of tradition and between the traditional and nontraditional ("religious" and "nonreligious") spheres of life. This segregation, however, is less total and rigid than that characterizing the first pattern. There tends to be more continuity between the different spheres, although this continuity does not ordinarily become fully formalized or ritualized. Usually, the members feel no strong predisposition toward rigid unifying principles, and so they tend to build up greater tolerance of ambiguity and of cognitive dissonance. They also accept the new symbols as the major collective referents of their personal identity. These symbols provide templates for guiding participation in the social and cultural order and lend meaning to many of the new institutional activities.

The groups or elites exhibiting this pattern tend to distinguish between different layers of traditional symbols to which commitments are maintained and to draw on all of them, insofar as possible, in the development of new tasks and activities. The first of these layers is that of certain basic modes of perception of the cosmic, cultural, and social orders. The second consists of the autonomous symbols of the collective identities of major subgroups and collectivities, however great may be the concrete changes in their content. Such groups may transpose traditional symbols into new, broader frameworks and may generate new, central symbols of personal or collective identity.

In this second pattern, however, either noncoercive or coercive elites may come to power, and their approaches produce major differences. Noncoercive elites tend to encourage the rise of new groups or collectivities, especially the more differentiated, specialized ones committed to new institutional goals. As a result, continuity of tradition may be maintained mostly in terms of general orientations, but not of full commitment to their content, which may continuously change. With a coercive elite, the situation is more complex.

Once in power, it is in a position to destroy most of the concrete symbols and structures of existing traditions, strata, and organizations and to emphasize a new content and new types of social organization. At the same time, however, it may preserve considerable continuity of certain basic modes of symbolic and institutional orientations. Coercive elites attempt to unleash, and at the same time to control in a new way, the primary motivational orientations inherent in the older systems, while changing their content and basic identity.

These various types of reconstitution of tradition and their possible relations to social-organizational dimensions are analyzed by the authors in great richness of detail. The detail is important, for it illuminates processes of struggle that accompany such crystallization of tradition. The authors also present interesting material on the conditions that produce these various types of crystallization—especially on the internal solidarity of the elites and of groups that participate in the process. Their book thus makes an important contribution to the analysis of the linkage of the symbolic realm and the structural-organizational realm, particularly in situations of change.

S. N. Eisenstadt

The Eliezer Kaplan School
of Economics and Social Sciences
The Hebrew University

Acknowledgments

The chapters of this book are revised versions of essays that were originally self-contained. In the course of time, we came to realize that the essays were closely related, and we decided to integrate them by developing a number of theoretical issues that were implicit in the original versions. The authorship of the book is joint, and our names appear in alphabetical order.

The fieldwork upon which this book is based and the writing were largely financed by the Bernstein Fund for Research in Israel, which granted us research fellowships at the Department of Social Anthropology of Manchester University. Financial assistance from the Research Committee of the Faculty of Social Sciences of Tel Aviv University helped us to prepare the manuscript for publication. Professor Max Gluckman, who heads the Bernstein Fund for Research in Israel, helped us immeasurably and consistently, both intellectually and through his good friendship. Without him the book would not have been written. We are also indebted to Professor S. N. Eisenstadt, who has through the years encouraged our research, and whose preface to the book has contributed to its theoretical thrust. At different times Professor Gluckman was assisted by our colleague Professor E. Marx and by Dr. P. T. W. Baxter, both of whom made helpful comments on various occasions when we presented material to them. Other people who read portions of the draft and made specific helpful suggestions are: M. Aronof, Abner Cohen, Erik Cohen, M. Douglas, D. Emmett, A. L. Epstein, M. Fortes, E. Gellner, H. Goldberg, E. Halevi-Etzioni, D. Handelman, H. Jason, J. Katz, H. Lewis, L. Mars, N. Nevo, P. Palgi, J. Pettigrew, M. Sarell, A. Weingrod, and S. Weitman. We also thank the participants of the various discussion groups and seminars to which we presented parts of the data: the field seminars in Israel of the Bernstein Fund, the staff seminars of the Department of Sociology and Anthropology of Tel Aviv University and the Hebrew University in Jerusalem, the folklore section of the World Congress of Jewish Studies in Jerusalem in 1969, the Tenth International Conference for the Sociology of Religion in Rome in 1969, the Seventh World Congress of Sociology in Varna in 1970, and the Association of Social Anthropologists Conferences in London in 1971, and in Canterbury in 1972. We were assisted by Mrs. A. Sommer (Goldberg), who helped with editing and styling, and by Mrs. D. Shai and Miss B. Fainberg.

Parts of the book have appeared in earlier versions as articles in journals and books. We are grateful for permission to reproduce, in revised form, the following copyrighted material: Moshe Shokeid, "Fieldwork as Predicament rather than Spectacle," *Archives européenes de sociologie* 12 (1971), 111–122; Shlomo Deshen, "On Religious Change: The Situational Analysis of Symbolic Action," *Comparative Studies in Society and History* 12 (1970), 260–274; "The Varieties of Abandonment of Religious Symbols," *Journal for the Scientific Study of Religion* 11 (1972), 33–41; and "Ethnicity and Citizenship in the Ritual of an Israeli Synagogue," *Southwestern Journal of Anthropology* 28 (1972), 69–82. Plates 1–5 are copyrighted by Werner Braun. Moshe Shokeid took photographs 6 and 7.

We are especially indebted to the people we studied, and are moved by respect and affection toward them. In the course of our fieldwork, they extended their hospitality and friendship, and subsequently we published our research and built academic careers upon it. We now hope that this book will contribute to their own and others' respect for their society. We have tried to portray them in their full humanity, showing not only their weaknesses but also their courage in facing the predicament of homecoming, the uncertainties of an unknown future in an unknown homeland. For the sake of the privacy of our informants, we use pseudonyms throughout, and we disguise the names of the places where they live. We dedicate the book to these people as an expression of our feelings.

SHLOMO DESHEN and MOSHE SHOKEID

Tel Aviv

THE PREDICAMENT OF HOMECOMING
Cultural and Social Life of
North African Immigrants in Israel

Introduction

SHLOMO DESHEN and MOSHE SHOKEID

> Who has heard such a thing?
> Who has seen such things?
> Is a land born in one day?
> Is a nation born at once?
> For as soon as Zion travailed
> She brought forth her children!
> —Isaiah 66:8

North African Jews are newcomers to Israel. Prior to the establishment of the state of Israel in 1948, they were to be found only in small communities in the traditional holy cities of Jerusalem and Tiberias and possibly in one or two other localities. Since 1948, however, when Jews began to immigrate in large numbers, North Africans have become a large and visible element in the Israeli population, numbering over 400,000 in a total Jewish population of over 2.7 million. The Israeli North Africans originate, in the main, from Morocco (about 230,000); about 70,000 are from Tunisia, and the remainder from the other countries of the region.[1]

Until recent generations the immigrants in North Africa lived mostly in a traditional environment, mainly in closely knit communities of relatives, and the household unit was

[1] The figures include both the immigrants and their Israeli-born children. They are perforce impressionistic, because official Israeli statistics give only the figures for the immigrant generation. For the purposes of this book, however, we attempt to cite figures based on a more realistic conception of Israeli ethnicity. The numbers could possibly be higher.

31

often coterminous with the extended family. The economic tasks and social position of Jews in the Moslem societies in which they lived had changed very little in the course of many generations. In the last few centuries they had been very much cut off from the Jewish communities in other parts of the world and from Jewish culture as developed there. The cultural development of North African Jews was further affected by the relatively stagnant societies in which they lived, societies not much influenced by Western intellectual movements and technology. Such movements were either unknown or foreign to them, and religion was the main area for cultural expression.

As a consequence of the establishment of French rule in North Africa (Algeria in 1830, Tunisia in 1881, Morocco in 1912), many facets of traditional society either disappeared or changed radically. However, the winds of change coming from Europe were felt very differently by the Jewish communities in the various parts of North Africa. Algerian Jewry was affected most profoundly by reason of the relatively long period of exposure to French influence. Nineteenth-century French policy toward the indigenous Algerian population was aimed specifically at attracting the Jews to the French rulers and to their culture while alienating the Moslem majority. This led to a weakening of traditional Jewish culture. By the turn of the century Algerian Jewish culture was already much less rich and vital than that of Moroccan and Tunisian Jewry, where in comparison traditional Jewish learning and piety flourished. As a result, Algerian Jewry has moved much closer than other Jewries of the region toward westernization and ultimately toward assimilation. It is, therefore, not surprising that when the position of Jews in Algeria became untenable in the 1960s, they by and large chose to make their home in France, rather than in Israel, where most of the other North African Jews migrated.

The French in Morocco and Tunisia, who had arrived more recently, had no policy that favored the Jewish population; consequently Jewish culture in those countries was affected far less. In the main, Jewish culture there remained vital and to an extent scholarly. Western culture did, however, penetrate it.

The Jewish communities of the northern coastal areas underwent significant changes in culture, livelihood, and domestic life. In the south, however, life continued very much as it had before the French came. In the remote Atlas Mountains of Morocco, people were only intermittently aware that there were new rulers in distant Casablanca, and French rule in that region was not effective till the 1930s. In the Tunisian island of Djerba and in the nearby villages of southern Tunisia there was possibly a little more awareness of the French, but their influence was yet minimal. The Franco-Jewish Alliance Israélite Univèrselle attempted to modernize Jewish schooling in Djerba in the late nineteenth century, but their efforts were strenuously and successfully resisted by the local community. From then on, southern Tunisian Jews were suspicious and hesitant about any changes emanating from the north. This attitude was bolstered by a history of ancient rivalries and disputes between the Jewish communities of northern and southern Tunisia.[2] Under these circumstances, whatever practical effect French culture might have had in southern Tunisia, it was of a most subtle nature and was cer-

[2] For historical background see such studies as Hirschberg 1965, Chouraqui 1972, Flamand n.d., Bensimon-Donath 1968, also our own attempts (in Deshen 1965 and Shokeid 1971b, ch. 2).

tainly not marked by dramatic overt changes, such as had occurred in Algeria and also, to some extent, in the large cities
of Morocco and Tunisia.

In this book we shall mostly be concerned with people
who originate from the more remote, traditional, southern
provinces. French culture was generally beyond their hori-
zon. With but one partial exception (to be described in
Chapter 7), none of the people discussed here were conversant, let alone literate, in French. Many of them did not
know a word of the language. And in their reminiscences of
the past, with which the people we studied often regaled us,
the French hardly figured. The same is true also of recent
collections of North African folk tales (Noy 1964, 1968):
there is hardly mention of the French. Thus, for all practical
purposes of the present study, we feel that one does not dis-
tort the picture by referring to the North African Jewish
background in terms of a traditional society.

Within a period of just over a decade, in the 1950s and
1960s, the age-old Jewish communities of North Africa
ceased to exist. The renascence of Jewish statehood attracted
masses of traditionalist Jews to Israel during the years that
immediately followed the creation of the state in 1948, while
the increasing nationalism and bigotry of North African
Moslems caused the enforced departure of the more assimi-
lated Jews a few years later. In 1971 there were only 1,000
Jews left in Algeria, 9,000 in Tunisia and about 40,000 in
Morocco, according to Israeli government sources. In 1948
the comparable figures were: 130,000 (Algeria), 110,000
(Tunisia), and 286,000 (Morocco). The case of the Jews in
the other countries of North Africa is similar.

The Judaic prophetic vision of the ingathering of exiles and
the renascence of Jewish sovereignty, which had been alive

with the Jewish people throughout two millennia and was now on the verge of realization, had fired the imagination of many North African Jews and had been the impetus of their immigration. The realities that they subsequently encountered in Israel, however, were at variance with the Jerusalem of their messianic vision. In Israel the immigrants had to cope with environmental, social, and cultural factors which often undermined their cultural norms and beliefs, their patterns of social relationships, and their group identity and image. They had to cooperate with new social groups and to adjust to different tasks and goals for economic and social achievements. Immigrants from North Africa, in common with immigrants from other Moslem countries, faced many problems in Israel.

In Israel the immigrants from North Africa became part of a larger society of Jews in which they were identified according to their country of origin. Thus instead of their previous identity as "Jews" among Moslems, they now became "Tunisians," "Moroccans," and so forth. This new ethnic identity was usually disadvantageous to them and often implied a lower cultural, economic, and social position vis-à-vis other Jewish ethnic groups. The immigrants also had to integrate into a society in which there were both agnostics and Jews whose patterns of ritual were different from their own. In the new environment, religion was no longer the main criterion and expression of Jewish life, and religious leaders did not hold the major positions in daily life. It was a society in which the Western scientific world was challenging and eroding long-established beliefs and mores in various spheres of life.

Furthermore, while previously the immigrants had been mainly peddlers and craftsmen, they now had to adjust to new forms of industrial, farming, and commercial activities and roles. Important economic resources, such as farmland, equipment, houses, and credit, as well as employment, were allocated to immigrants by various governmental agencies. All newcomers were entitled to equal rights and an equal share in all that the new society had to offer. They could carve out a new way of life and reach a better standard of living and a higher social position by competing for the resources at hand. They could, however, also survive without taking any initiative and subsist only on the elementary needs provided by public social services. In order to get a better share of the resources available, they often had to compete with other ethnic groups or with their own countrymen. They could compete and proclaim their demands as individuals, but they could also organize in different types of groupings for that purpose, such as kinship groups, factions, and ethnic associations.

Another set of problems was rooted in the "melting pot" ideology that prevailed among the absorption authorities during the years of mass immigration that lasted until the mid 1950s. This ideology, often reinforced by practical exigencies, frequently led to administrative decisions whereby groups of relatives and former communities were dispersed throughout various, and often remote, villages and towns. Nevertheless, immigrants could try to reunite their groups and communities in spite of administrative decisions. Dispersed or not, many immigrants often had to come to terms with a situation in which economic and social pressures, conflicting interests, and varying opportunities stimulated by the conditions of their new environment, caused community and family links to fall apart. These problems were compounded

by the general changes that the social order of the transplanted immigrant communities was undergoing. Some of
those who in North Africa had been rich and powerful lost
their wealth and esteem. On the other hand those who had
been poor and on a lower social rung could take advantage of
the new situation and improve their economic and social
position vis-à-vis their former superiors. Readjustment of attitudes and social relationships between individuals and
groups under these changes were difficult and often painful.
More specifically, to take up just one point within this broad
range of problems, factors operating in the new environment
of the immigrants often affected beliefs and attitudes even
within the framework of the nuclear family. One example is
the change in the status of women. The staffs of the agencies
dealing with the immigrants treated women as equals; moreover, many staff members were women. Compulsory education applied equally to boys and girls. Immigrant women
worked on farms, in industry, and in domestic service for
wages. Sometimes they adjusted better than the men to the
new kind of occupation, and their labor was in demand.
Another important factor affecting relationships within the
nuclear family was the dissolution of the extended family.

Many of the immigrants faced these problems and found
viable and suitable solutions. For them, life in Israel produced material, cultural, and personal rejuvenation—a
straightening of shoulders and raising of heads. Many others,
however, found life in Israel deeply frustrating and became
tragically disillusioned. Placed low on the socioeconomic ladder, they lacked significant power beyond the level of local
politics. On occasion, Moroccans have been prominent in
demonstrations and riots, a fact that helps to explain their

rather poor public image. Yet the majority of immigrants can be placed at various points between these two extremes of rejuvenation and profound disillusionment.

Those immigrants whose aspirations have not materialized in Israel, or who are otherwise frustrated, present one of the most serious current social problems in Israel. Though we are aware of this problem, we do not approach it frontally in this book. Instead, we deal with a number of major issues that struck us as extremely important in the general process of confronting new and conflicting social and cultural demands and constraints. The discussion is devoted mainly to analysis of how the people studied express, through symbolic action, their new experiences and the difficulties and the changes they have undergone in various spheres of life.

We argue that while the immigrants express their new experiences in the idiom of their traditional cultural symbols, they effect various changes in that traditional idiom and thereby cause mutation of their culture. This argument we develop by describing and discussing cultural and social activities in various situations. Two chapters are devoted to religious pilgrimages and trace specific variations of symbolism in pilgrimage activities that are interrelated with the exigencies of life and the changing social positions of the actors. Another two chapters deal with ceremony and belief within domestic and family contexts. Here we discuss emerging supernatural beliefs concerning relationships between spouses. These beliefs are shown to be interrelated with certain new conceptions and actions, specifically in the field of medicine, and with the division of labor between men and women. Also described are the seasonal gatherings of kinsmen and novel tendencies in ceremony with the accompanying social stresses that emerge in relationships between kin. The central theme of the book is further developed in chapters on synagogal ritual. Various mutations of the ritual are described and discussed within the context of the changing cultural and social environment.

We challenge implicitly in these studies various schools of thought that have sought to understand the phenomena of symbolic change in what we consider to be simplistic terms. We feel that little new light is shed on a phenomenon when discussed in the frame of such blanket concepts as "acculturation," "modernization," "culture change," or "revitalization." We seek in these studies to approach symbolic phenomena in terms that are more specifically suited to the analysis of symbolic action. At the same time we maintain an institutional-societal focus on the phenomena and remain committed to a structuralist-functionalist position in the broadest sense of the term.

The fieldwork on which this book is based was carried out mainly from the late summer of 1965 to the early spring of 1967. Deshen worked among immigrants from southern Tunisia in the town referred to as Ayara; Chapters 7 and 8 are based on this work. During that period he also worked among Moroccan immigrants in the town (Chapter 5) and southern Tunisian immigrants in other Israeli localities (Chapter 3). Shokeid's work was among immigrants from Morocco in the village referred to as Romema and his contributions to this book are all based on the Romema data. His earlier research, referred to in the book, was also carried out in immigrant villages in Israel.

Ayara, a provincial town whose population is composed mostly of new arrivals to the country, was founded in 1956 in a semiarid region. New immigrants were assigned homes in the town by the responsible immigration absorption authorities. In 1965 the town had about 17,000 inhabitants. Out of a total working-age population of 5,500, about 500 were employed on a seasonal or daily basis as unskilled agricultural workers on farms near the town. Approximately another 500 subsisted either on welfare or on relief work especially arranged for the elderly or handicapped. These two categories formed the lowest socioeconomic stratum. Besides these, and in a higher income bracket, were 1,800 persons employed in factories, 750 in tertiary services, 230 in commerce, and about 1,000 in the building trade and in other crafts.

The North Africans, 8,000 from Morocco and 1,700 from Tunisia, constituted over half the population of the town. The rest originated from other countries: over 4,000 were recent immigrants from eastern Europe and about 1,700 were people of European origin who had lived a long time in the country. There were also smaller groups from other parts of the world. On the whole, life for the people of Ayara was not easy. All of them were newcomers to the town, if not to the country. They had to adjust to different conditions, learn a new language, and interact with peoples of unfamiliar background. Though the whole population was Jewish, the immigrants felt themselves to be strangers in the country and in many ways to each other. People also had to adjust to the administrative and technical routines of the locale. These could be and were influenced and molded by the newcomers, yet the sensation of being foreigners, at least during the first years in the country, was very profound. Finally and most important, basic economic and housing conditions were often very trying, particularly for large families living in small cramped dwellings and having to make do on a meager income. We shall be considering mainly that part of the Ayara population which forms the lower socioeconomic stratum of the town. The breadwinners of these low-income families were usually unskilled laborers, and families tended to have many children, sometimes six and more, which further depressed their standard of living.

Romema is a village in the semiarid zone of the northern Negev. Like most other rural settlements of immigrants, Romema was planned by the settlement authorities [3] according to the *moshav* pattern. This type of settlement had been introduced into Israel in the 1920s by young European Jewish pioneers who wanted to establish a new society and a new social way of life. The *moshav* is an agricultural settlement organized on the basis of moderate economic and social cooperation (in comparison with the extreme form of the *kibbutz*). Each family cultivates its own farm and privately owns its own household and farm equipment. The farms and the houses in the *moshav* were planned to provide for a relatively small family unit which in turn was expected to be its own and sole source of labor. The nation owns the land, and each farmer is allocated the same facilities and amount of land by the national institutions which are administratively in charge. While the *moshav* ideology intends its members to remain economic equals, in practice economic differentiation may occur as a result of individual efforts, enterprise, and skills, as well as of familial demographic factors. Economic cooperation takes place in many important activities, such as the marketing of agricultural products, the supplying of farm

---

[3] The absorption of immigrants on the land was decided upon by the settlement authorities which were the government, the Jewish Agency, and the Settlement Movements (central institutions of settlers living in veteran villages of different political orientation). A network of complex organizations was set up in a short time to execute the process of absorption.

and household needs, and the sharing of such services as dairies and granaries. The most important administrative organs are the village committee and the general assembly; there are also many other committees with specific and limited functions. Members of committees and the incumbents of all offices are elected democratically every year. This pattern of settlement, although highly complicated and ideologically oriented, was considered to be the most suitable for absorbing the type of immigrant (mostly from Middle Eastern and North African countries) who has come to Israel since 1948.[4]

The settlers of Romema had come from a Jewish community, which we have called Amran, in the Atlas Mountains near Demnate. Its inhabitants, about sixty families, made their living mainly through a few specialized services for the Berbers: they were craftsmen—such as shoemakers, carpenters, smiths, and tailors—and peddlers of a few semi-industrial goods, such as sugar, candles, and oil. Some of the inhabitants of Amran helped to finance the Berbers' farms and herds, whose products they later shared and traded in nearby market towns. It was natural for a son to follow his father's occupation, especially since he had little other choice. Those in the community who had neither craft skills nor property usually served the more prosperous members, either by working in their businesses or in domestic service. They lived almost entirely within the fold of the Jewish culture which they had inherited and which had been kept alive mainly through an oral tradition handed down from generation to generation. Because of the isolation of Amran, this

---

[4] For a more complete description of the social and economic basis and problems of the *moshav* see Ben-David 1964, Weingrod 1966, Weintraub *et al.* 1969, Shokeid 1971b.

tradition had not been greatly influenced by the mainstreams of Jewish culture developed in other parts of the Diaspora in recent centuries.

One of the more important religious activities in Amran was the reading of the Zohar; these reading sessions were held regularly in small groups. The Zohar, a Jewish gnostic work of the thirteenth century, was believed to have been written by Rabbi Shimeon bar Yohai [5] (the pilgrimage to his tomb will be described in Chapter 2). The text is esoteric, and though the readings were difficult to understand, they aroused strong feelings of sacredness and piety. The Jews believed that mystic powers were evoked through the reading of the Zohar which could cure the sick (for whose sake a special session might be held) and, more generally, which sustained the existence of the community. Belief in spirits, demons, and the evil eye was widespread.

In 1956 the entire population of Amran migrated to Israel; and in 1957 thirty-three families settled in Romema. On their arrival there, the settlers resolved into three main family groups, which were soon involved in fierce competition for positions in the village administration and for economic resources.

Not until 1963 were plots of thirty-five dunams (seven acres) of irrigated land and farming equipment allocated to each family (defined as a married couple, with or without children), when the settlers began to farm assiduously. Until then the Romemites had worked as laborers on farms and in orchards of neighboring villages and in other occupations

---

[5] Critical examination of the *Zohar* fails to substantiate the assumption. The dominant view in modern scholarship is that it is the work of Rabbi Moses de Leon (d. 1305) and that it was written around 1270 (see Scholem 1955, Chapters 5 and 6).

connected with agriculture. Since they began independent farming, many Romema settlers have acquired a reputation for hard work and successful farming. They exhaust all the means available to them: generally they use up their entire quotas for water and crops [6] and exploit their land to the fullest. Moreover, an increasing number of farmers have begun to farm additional plots of land which have not yet been allocated to settlers or on which permanent irrigation pipes have not yet been installed. Since 1965 most of the people of Romema have enjoyed an economic boom, in contrast to their earlier experience in Israel and in contrast to some of the other villagers in the region and immigrants settled in nearby provincial towns (Ayara included).

We come now to the specific chapters that make up this book. In Chapter 1, Shokeid describes his personal field situation and the problems he encountered as he forged for himself a role in the field. The problems faced by the anthropologist who studies a segment of his own society as well as the professional advantages of such a field situation run through the chapter. Shokeid emphasizes the sense of commitment and obligation toward the studied society. Synagogal ritual, memorial celebrations, and the activities of a group of Moroccan immigrant villagers in that context are portrayed in Chapter 2. Here Shokeid seeks to understand the particulars in the changing patterns of religious actions (that is, the emergence of trends of ascetic behavior) in terms of changes

[6] Since the sources of water in the country, especially in the Negev area, are limited, every village is entitled to a specified yearly quota of water. This quota is equally divided among the settlers. In order to avoid saturation of the market of any particular product, each village in Israel is permitted to cultivate a limited acreage of each crop or to produce a limited amount of eggs, poultry, meat, or dairy products. The quota of the village should be divided equally among its settlers.

in the system of social stratification and social relationships in a transplanted immigrant community. In Chapter 3, by Deshen, the focus shifts to Tunisian immigrants in an urban setting who also engage in memorial celebrations. As in the study of Moroccan immigrants' celebrations, the author indicates various aspects of the celebrations that are new developments among Tunisian immigrants. These are analyzed as religious responses to certain problems peculiar to the immigrant situation. The memorial celebrations became popular precisely at a time when political ethnicity in Israel seemed to be recessing, while during the years when political ethnicity was very much in evidence in Israel such memorial celebrations held little attraction for the North African immigrants. While Shokeid tackles the problem of religious change in terms of the changing institutional structure of the community, Deshen approaches the problem from the point of view of the phenomenological nature of the religious actions. Far from considering our different approaches to be contradictory, we believe that they complement each other, and that further effort should be expended to wed these two approaches.

The confrontation between traditional beliefs on male barrenness and Western medical diagnosis and treatment is analyzed in Chapter 4 by Shokeid. This confrontation sublimated barrenness into a problem viewed in supernatural terms, whereas traditionally it had been considered in pragmatic terms. The new form in which the nature of barrenness was apprehended led to the emergence of novel supernatural ways of handling and interpreting the problem of the physical inadequacy of the male who traditionally was not held responsible for barrenness. This is contiguous to the problem of finding answers to new overwhelming experiences in personal, cultural, and social life, discussed through the analyses of the appearance of series of new actions and modes of behavior in memorial celebrations.

The problem of religious changes is taken up by Deshen in Chapters 5 and 6 in more precise technical terms. Being concerned with the phenomenological nature of religion, Deshen develops a typology of religious changes according to shifts in the relationships between the elements that constitute the religious actions. The ethnographic basis of the argument in Chapter 5 is taken from observations in an urban Moroccan synagogue; in Chapter 6, where the argument is further developed, it is based on observations in a Tunisian synagogue in the same town. In Chapter 7, Deshen examines a series of religious actions in a Tunisian synagogue which elucidates and substantiates his approach to religious change; he concludes that these actions are relevant to the forging of interethnic and civic bonds.

In "The Evolution of Kinship Ties among Moroccan Immigrants," Chapter 8, Shokeid describes the seasonal reunion of people who emigrated from one village in Morocco and were dispersed in Israel. According to the analysis of the data, the loosening of kinship bonds and the weakening of familial considerations in social action are compensated by and symbolized through the intensity of the ceremonial at gatherings of relatives.

This chapter, which concludes the book, is the study of a situation that represents dramatically the achievements, the failures, the fate and the predicament of the people we studied, in their various localities, since immigration to Israel.

CHAPTER 1

Involvement Rather than Spectacle in Fieldwork

MOSHE SHOKEID

A student in the British anthropological tradition, I was confronted with the problem of partial commitment to, and only partial detachment from, the people I studied, when for eighteen months I observed a group of Jews from the Atlas Mountains, to whom I was in some ways a foreigner and in others not (Shokeid 1971b). They had immigrated to Israel in 1956 and had settled in a cooperative village (to which I gave the name Romema). As a Jew born in Israel, into a family which had come from eastern Europe about half a century earlier, I was intrigued by the mass exodus of Jews from many countries to Israel which took place after 1948, particularly by the immigrants from the Middle East and North Africa. The social, cultural, and ideological background of those Jews was very different from that of most of the veteran population in Israel, who originated mainly from eastern and central Europe.[1] It was my great curiosity, therefore, to know about people with whom I have a common bond of ancient history and recent citizenship that prompted me to study the Atlas Mountains Jews. I wanted to know about their culture, manners, and social life, the vision they

[1] See Minkovitz (now Shokeid) 1967a.

had had of their ancient homeland while in their native country, and the ways in which they came to terms with their new physical, economic, social, and cultural environment. Therefore, unlike anthropologists who study societies other than their own, I was not as naturally detached from my field.

Although in many respects I was different from the settlers of Romema (whom I shall henceforth call Romemites), I was in their eyes a Jew and an Israeli like themselves. As Israelis, we were all confined to a relatively tiny territory and a small population in which one cannot indefinitely maintain social anonymity or escape communication with others. This basic social and physical proximity obliged me, during my fieldwork and afterward, to confront challenges, pressures, and problems which, I believe, are not familiar to most anthropologists, who are complete strangers and outsiders to the societies which they study.

A moving description by Turner of his last meeting with one of his informants illustrates a fairly typical relationship between anthropologists and the members of the societies which they study: [2] "Shortly before I left his land, probably for ever, he [the informant] came to see me and we had an outwardly cheerful drink together; presently, he grew quiet, then said: 'When your motor car sets out in the early morning do not expect to see me nearby. When somebody dies we Ndembu do not rejoice, we have a mourning ceremony' " (Turner 1960:354). The foreign anthropologist and his close informant from an African tribal society are likely to part forever. The case seems to demonstrate that the greater the sympathy and the closer the relationship between the anthro-

---

[2] See also Paul 1953, Frankenberg 1963, Maquet 1964, Barnes 1967, Köbben 1967, Hofer 1968, Baxter n.d.

pologist and his hosts, the more noteworthy and poignant the knowledge that they must inevitably part.

During fieldwork the foreign anthropologist often seems to become integrated into his host society, especially when he fraternizes with a particular kinship group (see Paul 1953, Baxter, n.d.). Yet neither he nor his hosts are deceived by this. The anthropologist continues to be an outsider, since he remains very different from the members of his host society, who know and comprehend little about his social roots.[3] To them the anthropologist is like a visitor from another planet to which he will eventually return.[4] This type of situation enables the social anthropologist to sustain a remarkable degree of detachment and objectivity in his observation of, and relation to, the subjects of his study. At the same time, he can be relatively comfortable about the degree of his commitment to his host society. He is not expected to conform to the norms of the society he studies. He should, of course, show respect for the local customs and beliefs, which he is only too ready to do since it gives him access to the necessary means of observation and information. But the relationship of the anthropologist to his studied society on the level of conscientious responsibility usually ends with his departure—the studied society then becomes for him an accumulation of data.[5]

While "other" societies have been the main concern of anthropologists, both in the United States and in Europe, there

[3] See Firth's discussion (1936) on the limits of the anthropologist's absorption into the native surroundings.

[4] For a more specialized analysis on the role of the outsider anthropologist, see Vidich 1955.

[5] Maybury-Lewis (1965) is an example of the complexity faced by those anthropologists who study "other" societies and try to carry over their conscientious responsibility after they leave their field of research.

always were those who carried out researches inside their own society.[6] The number is increasing, particularly in the developing states. M. N. Srinivas, who has done such research for many years in India,[7] has been joined by others.

A number of decisive and specific factors have prompted anthropologists to turn more and more to subjects of study within their own society. First, the original drive behind the study of primitive societies to provide evidence for the elementary forms of social institutions and for the relativity of social norms has gradually decreased. Second, primitive societies are quickly disappearing, mainly because of the process of "modernization" and "westernization." More important, however, seems to be the fact that these societies are undergoing change, emerging as the new nations of the "third world," and their elite does not seem to be well disposed toward alien social anthropologists. As pointed out by Maquet (1964) and Lévi-Strauss (1966b), the social anthropologists either are identified with the former colonials or are accused of degrading the indigenous populations of the new nations through their studies, in which, the elite claims, the natives are presented as primitive people. Finally, it seems to me that the anthropologist is turning to his own society for study in the context of Western societies' current search for their own identities and Western man's increasing discontent with his social conditions. The recent expansion of schools of sociology in British universities seems to me to be one indication of this trend in anthropological studies. If it flourishes and develops into an actual phase of anthropological study,

---

[6] See for instance West 1945, Frankenberg 1957, 1963.

[7] See particularly Srinivas' own evaluation of his position as expressed in the essay "Some Thought on the Study of One's Own Society" (Srinivas 1966).

anthropologists will inevitably face a new field situation, with new relationships with the studied communities, both during and after the period of fieldwork. He will find that the classic situation of noncommitment no longer holds, and he will be confronted by the challenges, as well as the problems, involved in a situation of relative commitment.

Lévi-Strauss, in contending that the main reasons for a crisis in social anthropology are the alleged imminent disappearance of primitive societies and the rejection of social anthropologists by the new nations, concludes: "When social anthropology is practised by members of the culture which it endeavours to study, anthropology loses its specific nature and becomes rather akin to archaeology, history and philology. For anthropology is the science of culture as seen from the outside" (1966b:126).[8] While I do believe that anthropologists can study their own culture, I concur with Lévi-Strauss' view that "anthropology is the science of culture as seen from the outside," since I believe that studies in anthropology, as well as sociology, can properly be carried out only by persons who, despite the fact that they "belong," are in some ways outsiders in their own society: they have the quality to perceive their own society from a vantage point of detachment. If one is able to notice and analyze the peculiarities of other societies but cannot objectively view the idiosyncrasies in his own society, his judgments lack the objectivity that anthropologists claim. I strongly believe that the test of anthropology, and probably its future perspectives, depend on the ability of anthropologists to carry out studies in their own society. This does not necessarily imply

[8] A somewhat similar argument was also raised by Leach (1963) in his discussion on Srinivas' cited work. He posed the question "How far can any sociologist understand his own society?" (p. 377).

the study of one's immediate social environment, such as one's own lineage, village, or class. All societies, whether modern ones or those labeled at present as primitive, are heterogeneous enough to provide their own social outsiders (see Srinivas 1966). Thus our discussion is mainly concerned with two interrelated issues: (a) the extent of the anthropologist's commitment and responsibility toward the people he studies; (b) the scope of anthropology when practiced by members of the studied societies.

I will now describe some of the trials I underwent, and some of the possible errors that I made. These, I think, will illuminate a situation which many other anthropologists may face in the future, although the particular forms will be different.

Problems of Involvement and Commitment

The first main practical and moral problem that confronted me was connected with the religious behavior Romemites expected of me. The Romemites are highly traditional and religious, while I am an agnostic. It is important to realize that Jewish tradition as perpetuated and interpreted by the Romemites is very intolerant toward those Jews who do not conform to prescribed religious behavior. I soon realized that the scope of my work, as well as my acceptance, would be influenced by the extent of my readiness to conform, overtly at least, to Jewish religious norms. To adopt the role of the pious was a difficult step to take. I was mainly uneasy about cheating and also afraid of the danger of being "caught in the act." Technically, I could cope with this role during ritual, because of my previous experience among Orthodox Jews. The knowledge I gained then stood me in good stead now. In ritual I also quickly learned to imitate with ease the

actions and movements of the other worshipers. My occasional faux pas were looked upon with good humor because
of my background, which the Romemites thought was rooted
in Ashkenazi traditions (variants of Jewish tradition and customs that developed in medieval central and northern
Europe; also used when referring to adherents thereof). I
tried not to trespass any of the Sabbath precepts, and I observed taboos concerning food, and so forth. In the synagogue, however, whenever I was called up to take an honor-
ary part in the procedure of reading from the Scrolls of the
Law, I fumbled in embarrassment. I did my best to avoid
these honors, and my refusals were taken, to my further discomfort, as signs of my modesty. This hardly meant that nobody noticed my clumsiness; in fact, the rabbi, himself an
outsider to the community and of doubtful status among his
congregation, sensed my uneasiness during ritual activities.

Eventually, however, the Rabbi grew less reserved toward
me. On an occasion celebrating the acquisition of some books
of religious content by a Romemite, he asked the audience to
give a toast in my honor. He explained that they should
thank God for the good fortune of having me in Romema
since I exemplified the traditional value expressed in the rabbinical saying *derekh-eretz kadma la'Torah*, namely, that the
duty of *derekh-eretz* preceded the Torah (the Pentateuch) by
twenty-six generations (Midrash Rabbah, Leviticus 9:3).
Derekh-eretz literally means "way of the land." It is a difficult
term to render, connoting, among other meanings, the traditional ideals of proper conduct in relation to other people:
modesty, truthfulness, consideration and respect toward others, ethical behavior, and so forth. According to the adage,
the duty of *derekh-eretz* started with Adam, the first man,
while the Torah, which mainly regulates the relationship be-

tween man and God, was not given until the time of Moses, twenty-six generations later. The acceptance of the Torah posits a priori the principles of *derekh-eretz*, namely, adopting the proper way of life on earth. This rabbinical saying is held up as a moral dictum on occasions of misconduct in social relationships, either by the learned and important or by the common people.

Romemites performed their religious duties scrupulously, but in their social relationships they were often discourteous to one another (sometimes also to strangers)—a failing that they lamented. In praising my *derekh-eretz* on this festive occasion, the rabbi pointed, without malice, at the deficiencies and merits in both myself and in the Romemites. I was grateful for the gesture; it signified that I had now merited my standing by the traditional value of proper behavior. At the same time my clumsiness in religious ritual was publicly accepted.

To summarize, I faced two major difficulties with regard to religious behavior. First, I was expected to be "Jewish," which in this case meant conforming to Jewish religious precepts. Second, in fulfilling this expectation, I had to face the possibility that one day, either during my fieldwork or afterward, my false pretenses might be discovered.

A more specific example of the pressure to conform to the Romemites' norms and expectations that I experienced may be demonstrated by the dilemma I faced at the Passover festival. During my stay in Romema, I had vouched as little information as I could about my family background and about my other social commitments and activities. It was known, however, that my parents lived in Tel Aviv. With the approach of Passover, I realized that according to the Romemites' custom the first day of the festival, on which the main

Passover feast takes place is regarded specifically as a family occasion and is celebrated in the close family circle. In sharp contrast to their behavior during other festivals, none of the Romemites was planning to celebrate the festival away from the nuclear family circle; similarly, no guests from the outside, relatives or friends, were expected to come to Romema for that day. Although I would definitely have been invited to celebrate the day with a number of the local families, I realized from casual talk and through some matter-of-fact remarks that it would have been in bad taste, and that it would have impaired my image, had I stayed. It would certainly have implied disrespect on my part toward my parents. Thus to preserve my image of a well-mannered Jew, I had to leave for the first day of Passover, in spite of my desire to stay.

Whatever the price, the mere possibility given to me to conform to some of the elementary values of my host society put me, I believe, in a better position to understand certain social and cultural aspects of that community. At times I felt that the Romemites were proud to have me with them, precisely because I was different in some ways and was identified with the veteran Ashkenazi prestigious sector of Israeli society. To the Romemites, my association with them, especially because of our close relationships, epitomized, to some extent, the aspirations toward integration of the returning exiles. They insisted that I partake as an equal of their food, particularly of their drinks, during Sabbath meals and on other occasions. This bestowal of equality to them became symbolic of the bridge that could span the social distance between us. My hosts' anxiety to stabilize our friendship beyond my role and stay of fieldwork often came to light in their hopes, frequently expressed during meals on the Sabbath, that I should soon be married. Their concern was often very touching. They once even tried to introduce me to a girl, a distant relative of some of the Romemites, whom they thought suitable to my status. She came from an urban background in Morocco and was better educated than the others. The Romemites expected me to marry partly in order to fulfill the traditional Jewish norms which one was duty bound to conform to at my age. (At the same time they assumed that Ashkenazi Jews, particularly those with a higher education, married late.) Mainly, I think, the Romemites had looked forward to the change in my family status to allow for the establishment of a reciprocal pattern of visiting and hospitality after my fieldwork. The Romemites did not expect me to settle in their village. They realized that eventually I would live near a university center, but wherever I resided, our relationship would have depended on whether or not I was married. The Romemites are used to traveling long distances in order to visit their relatives or close friends. Mutual visits are dominated by lavish, though often hurriedly prepared, meals, since the Romemites might visit or be visited without previous notice. Only a married man who could rely on his wife's efficiency and culinary abilities could participate fully, and on equal terms, in this pattern of expressing and practicing close relationships.

When I finally left the Romemites and went to England, we did not part forever. I was expected to return in due course to Israel, and we were bound to meet, for Israel is a country too small to permit final farewells.

My hosts gradually became aware that I would write about Romema and give their community some publicity. Although they had emigrated from an environment where education was rare, they had been brought up to respect learning and creativity in writing. At the beginning, they were embarrassed by the complexity of the situation and wanted to impress me with their Jewish cultural heritage and other achievements, since I represented the veteran section of the Israeli society and was in a position to make comparisons with other sections of immigrants. During the early stage of my stay, they were, therefore, sensitive about those aspects in their community life which they thought might spoil their reputation. Some of them, mainly those who had already established close relationships with me, occasionally asked me not to write about the disorder which I witnessed during the ritual proceedings in the synagogue. Later on, when my presence became part of the social scenery, they stopped commenting on this subject, presumably relying on my friendship and understanding.

When I started to write up the data, I was confronted with a heavy responsibility toward my hosts in Romema. The usual method of disguising the names of the village and the people mentioned, inadequate perhaps in other cases (see Barnes 1967), seemed to be even more so here, considering the smallness and density of the Israeli society. At the time of my fieldwork, one Romema boy was already attending an institution of higher learning and he might come across my works, even if published in English. I had to face the possibility—posed long ago by Whyte's pioneering study (1964 [1943]:279–356)—that the Romemites might be deeply offended by my records. They would not be able to consider the abstractions of social behavior, but would be mainly concerned with the narrative descriptions of their political, religious, and family behavior. These they would interpret as blemishes on their reputation and a betrayal on my part. In their struggle for social esteem among the different sectors of the Israeli society, the Romemites might blame my account for stripping and humiliating them in public. I could also be considered as representing the hypocrisy and seemingly high-handed manner of the veteran Ashkenazi Israeli stratum. For example, when I started to write up my field data, it was difficult for me to express in a straightforward way my hosts' intellectual background, knowing how vulnerable they were about it. Living for generations in the remote and lawless Atlas Mountains, almost completely isolated from the centers of Eastern and Western Judaism, had affected the Romemites culturally, and those who had come to Israel were obviously at an intellectual disadvantage in comparison with those in some other Jewish communities. Apparently objective facts which referred to a general local situation might seem offensive to the Romemites. My self-imposed responsibility toward the Romemites might, therefore, have led me to be somewhat predilect in the presentation of my study; whether this is so is difficult for me to judge. While writing up my data, however, I decided to adopt a new Hebrew surname, associated with the name of the village I studied. That decision gave me a sense of freedom in my writings about the Romemites since it represented to me, and I hoped would demonstrate to the villagers, the deep sympathy and respect I had for them. It is a common practice among people from all levels of society in Israel to choose Hebrew surnames to replace those their ancestors had adopted perhaps centuries before in Europe and elsewhere in the Diaspora. The new names are either translations of the old ones, or biblical names, or names of objects, as well as names related to events of personal significance. My new name, which was concrete proof of my association with the village, reduced my qualms and uneasiness in presenting my data. This act afforded me the means to satisfy both my anthropological passion and my professional responsibility to report in detail about the Romemites' behavior. I found out later that my acquaintances in Romema had been pleased by the change of my name.

The important observation to be made, however, lies in the action I was able to take within the limits of, and the opportunities offered to me by, the culture and norms of Israeli society. It appears to me as an example of many other types of cultural and social adaptation that different societies might offer in situations similar to my own.[9]

Anthropology by "Natives"

The second issue of the discussion is whether anthropology can be practiced by members of the studied society. There are obviously some elementary advantages and disadvantages in either being a foreigner or being a member of the society that one studies. It would, therefore, always be advantageous to have reports on any particular society from both types of researchers. They may complement each other's naïveté (see Hofer 1968), as well as compensate for the price paid either for commitment or for dissociation and detachment.

In my own case, I am convinced that my command of Hebrew and my familiarity with Jewish culture were decisive factors in my research, factors which also influenced my analysis.[10] They made accessible avenues which might otherwise have been closed to me. For example, I gradually came

---

[9] In this context see also Chaudhri's (Pettigrew's) account (1969) of the particular problems she had to cope with during fieldwork because of her affinal relationship with one group.

[10] See also arguments raised by Edit Fél and Tamás Hofer (1972), who studied in their own society.

to realize that when the Romemites tried either to impress their audience with their arguments, or to emphasize the importance of their subject, they sometimes used an archaic style of speech. This type of oratory, using the vocabulary, images, and grammatical constructions characteristic of the literary style of different historical periods, gave the impression that traditional sources were being referred to, and in this way the orator invested his statements with some authority. This realization on my part pointed to specific directions in analysis. Political life in Romema revealed to me a particular credo of egalitarianism which was derived from different social and cultural factors. I gained a keen insight into this phenomenon during a nocturnal debate by Romemites on the terms of nomination to a particular office in the village organization. The debaters had long and noisy arguments about the appropriate salary to be paid to the official. The discussion came to an end that evening when Yirmya Amzlag, one of the chief debaters, who had argued intensely against what he considered to be pretentious demands by the candidate to the office, challenged his opponents with the following phrase in his argument: "Haven't I a portion and a heritage (*heilek venahala*) in Eretz Yisrael (the Land of Israel)?" Nobody countered this last point and a minute of silence reigned. Noticing the murmur of approval running through the audience and realizing that his opponents were momentarily speechless, Yirmya left trimphantly for home. The phrase *heilek venahala* is common in biblical literature. In Yirmya's speech it implied the notion of the juridical equal right of every Jew to the benefits of Israel in general, and of Romema in particular. He actually reduced the discussion to the basic formula of their existence in the village, the relationship between Jews and Zion. By pointing to this basic relationship between the people of Romema, Yirmya proclaimed an egalitarianism which would have been violated by acceding to the proposed candidate's apparently exaggerated demands. In fact, he invoked the Exodus from Egypt and the very first settlement of the Jews in the Promised Land thousands of years ago. The Bible tells us that the Land of Israel was divided equally among the twelve tribes—descendants of Jacob, his other name being Israel (Yisrael)—and equal shares of tribal territory were accorded to every household (Numbers 26, 33, 34; Joshua 13–19).

In conclusion, Yirmya's last argument was a powerful manipulation of traditional symbols which touched on the deeper layers of the Romemites' cultural and religious convictions. An informant in this case would have had to produce a version much more complicated and expressive than a merely accurate translation. He would have had to interpret rather than record, and thus do the job of the anthropologist himself.

There seems to exist a false assumption that outsiders are by definition impersonal and objective. This assumption was critically dealt with by Maquet (1964), who argued, for example, that anthropological studies carried on in Africa were much influenced by the socioeconomic status of the anthropologists. Maquet suggests a value-free and stimulating way of tackling the problem of objectivity in the study of society:

Individual and social perspectives of an anthropologist are not easy to evaluate. A perspective knowledge is not as such non-objective: it is partial. It reflects an external reality but only an aspect of it; the one visible from the particular spot, social and individual, where the anthropologist was placed. Non-objectivity creeps in when the partial aspect is considered as the global one. Any knowledge, even that obtained through an impersonal subject, is partial, thus inadequate to the external reality. Several perspective views of the same social phenomenon help to describe more precisely each view point and consequently to determine how each of them affects the resulting knowledge. [1964:54]

We should remember in this context the discussion on Srinivas raised by Leach (1963). The fact that Srinivas is a Brahmin equipped him better to observe the phenomenon of "Sanskritization" in depth and in detail; it also probably prompted him toward the study. His intimate knowledge of Hinduism was a primary condition that allowed him, as an anthropologist, to study and follow this type of development. Srinivas' contribution to the subject is of great professional importance, even if it is influenced and biased by a "Brahminocentric" point of view, as argued by Leach. In the line of thinking suggested by Maquet, I believe that any sociological or anthropological analysis of social behavior includes some kind of individual conceptualization which cannot claim to be the only possible and objective one.

Finally, returning to the initial discussion of the anthropologist's commitment and responsibility, I would say that anthropology is presently at a disadvantage compared to sociology and psychology. The latter disciplines have long enjoyed legitimization from that same Western society which has always been their field of study. Anthropology, on the other hand, has concentrated until very recently on primitive groups, gaining legitimization through the intellectual curiosity and practical needs of the external Western society. The doubts which I have experienced and the eventual choices of action which I have made during my fieldwork and afterward were much influenced by the lack of institutionalized professional norms to help cope with the new situation in which the anthropologist is no longer a foreigner.

Theoretically, at least, one may assume that with the development of attitudes of introspection, communities will gradually become less sensitive and touchy about being analyzed. While the assumption is validly grounded, the fact remains that the majority of anthropological studies still have for their subjects the less sophisticated groups in any society. And these are even less prepared to be tolerant and are more sensitive to analysis than more sophisticated groups.

I have tried to point out some of the professional dilemmas which seem to emerge at the present transitional stage in the application of the anthropological method. No attempt was made to suggest a solution. I assume, however, that the professional institutionalization and legitimization of this phase of anthropology will be greatly influenced by the increasingly pertinent response of other involved anthropologists.

CHAPTER 2

An Anthropological Perspective on Ascetic Behavior and Religious Change

MOSHE SHOKEID

Sociologists of religion in the Weberian tradition have searched for compatibility and correlation between various spheres of life and religious movements. Revealingly, however, the Weberian view does not consider the sphere of individual behavior. Thus, while a particular ascetic ideology may be compatible with a particular economic and political ethos, or state of affairs, the theory which illuminates that correlation fails to explain why people choose and develop one specific ascetic ideology among other available ideologies. Are people motivated, for example, mainly by problems of ultimate meaning in ethics or metaphysics; or are their choices determined by and large by their social, political, and economic positions, interests, and aspirations? Subsequent developments of the correlation between religious behavior and economic or political phenomena are directly influenced by the nature of the motivation or of the situational constraints. Consequently, an examination of the correlation from different angles requires the study of the motivational and situational spheres. My query is thus similar to the query of those who criticized the functionalists for not taking into account the motivational dimension (for example, Bredmeier 1955, Homans and Schneider 1955). (Mention should here be made of Geertz [1962], Srinivas [1966], Long [1968], and Abner Cohen [1969], who in recent years have presented a more direct and immediate relation between religious behavior and economic and political interests and actions.)

In this chapter I hypothesize that a certain situational pattern motivates people to choose and develop a more ascetic ideology and way of life, though there are other alternatives. I shall argue that the adoption of ascetic ideals and an ascetic way of life may be closely related to the development of social differentiation or conflicting aspirations in society. In showing such a relation, however, I do not necessarily imply that the cleavages which emerge in society encourage the deprived groups to look for some kind of religious justification for the lower position they presently have in life. On the contrary, I demonstrate—a phenomenon reminiscent of Srinivas' observation of Sanskritization (1966)—that groups whose economic and political position has greatly advanced may choose ascetic norms and induce religious change. According to my analysis, asceticism may serve as a symbolic system that demonstrates changes in the structure of social differentiation and acts as a powerful means to elaborate further and to develop that differentiation or conflict.

While studying the people of Romema, I observed how some persons tried to assert through ritual their claims to differential status in terms of social changes which had occurred in other institutional spheres. That phenomenon raised the question whether the religious domain is able to absorb such claims and to answer the demands made. The members of that community, divided into a few groups of relatives, were continuously competing for prestige in the economic, political, and ritual spheres (Shokeid 1971b). In one of the groups,

I observed the emergence of new pietistic patterns and trends toward ascetic behavior, which were particularly noticeable in ritual. This phenomenon I identify as a new style of behavior in which the group singles out and emphasizes certain symbols from among the pool of accepted cultural symbols. The group in question therefore has to redefine the relative importance of certain norms and goals of achievement as well as the means of achieving them.

Among recent anthropological studies I mention here only Turner (1966), Shack (1968), and Boissevain (1969), who have demonstrated the phenomenon of competition for prestige during ritual. The competing participants in the rituals which they observed failed, however, to affirm and integrate new patterns of differential status. In contrast with the phenomena they studied, my data reveal a process of breakthrough which stimulates religious innovation and provides means for affirming differential status among the participants. (I shall later compare my data with that of Boissevain, who also studied a community practicing a universal religion.)

Ascetic movements and sects have developed at one time or another in all universal religions. One may assume that some of them have emerged on a small scale and then developed into large movements. It is beyond the scope and data of my discussion to find out what particular historical circumstances induce this process. Although the case I report will probably not develop into a wide religious movement, it provides, in my opinion, an insight into some possible structural features and processes conducive to religious change.

Social Structure and Competition

On their arrival in Romema in 1957, the settlers defined themselves, and were identified by others, as members of three groups of relatives, each known by the family name of the core members: Sebag, Biton, and Mahluf. Each of these core groups consisted, in the main, of kinsfolk plus a few members from other patronymic groups who had committed themselves by marriage or otherwise to one or another of the core groups. The groups were soon involved in competition, called "*hamulot* feuding" by outsiders, which term was also adopted by the Romemites. *Hamula* (singular) is a common term in the Middle East for an agnatic minimal lineage which is a corporate group. In the context of an Israeli immigrant society, this term is also applied to groups that do not necessarily conform to this definition.[1]

I have analyzed elsewhere (Shokeid 1971b) the relation between present rivalries among the Romemites and the social differentiation which existed in Amran, their community of origin in Morocco. In Amran, the Sebags, who had been wealthy merchants, had enjoyed a better economic and social position than had the Bitons, who had been mainly the poorer traveling craftsmen and the unskilled residents of the community. The Mahlufs had had an intermediate position: they had practiced crafts of higher skill and some of their members had been among the better-educated Amranites. In Romema the Sebags, according to my observations, tried to preserve their earlier superior position, while the Bitons tried to reverse the lowly position they had had in Amran. The

[1] For more details about the phenomenon of *hamulot* feuding in Israeli immigrants' villages, see Shokeid 1968.

Mahlufs gradually declined in number and they consequently played a lesser role. The Romemites competed in various spheres of life: (1) the economic; (2) the political—over leadership positions in the *moshav*; (3) in ritual.

Modes of Competition
In the Economic Sphere

The Romemites strove to get extra jobs, to expand their farming, and to acquire more and more material possessions. The Sebags, in particular, were increasing their farming activities beyond their entitled quota of land, water, and crops. The Bitons tried to keep up with the Sebags both by expanding their own farming and, as much as possible, by curtailing the expansion of the Sebags by enforcing *moshav* rules and sanctions against them. The two groups competed over the acquisition of farm and household equipment. Thus, for example, Levy Biton, one of the leading figures in his group, was the first person in Romema to own a tractor—it was of medium size and he managed it skillfully. Aziz Sebag, the oldest son of the last head of the Amran community, had for a long time also been considering buying a tractor together with his brothers. Although he was obviously incompetent with machinery, he eventually bought one of a bigger size on his own. Aziz also frequently spoke of the pleasures and the usefulness of having a car. But it was Levy Biton who first bought a van (in 1968). Levy also installed a solar heating apparatus for warming water although he had told me some time earlier that it would be an unwise investment (about IL. [Israeli pounds] 1,000 = $300). However, he felt that he had to get one because most of the Sebags had already installed them.

In the Political Sphere

The competition over key positions in the organization of the *moshav* (such as secretary, shopkeeper, produce marketer, rabbi, and so forth) was keen but abortive. The Bitons consistently rejected the candidates of the Sebags, and vice versa. Neither group would readily approve the candidate of the other group since approval might have been taken for acknowledgment of its own political and social inferiority. Most of the offices of the *moshav* organization of Romema were therefore filled by outsiders. But when the settlement authorities or circumstances forced the settlers to nominate a Romemite to one of the offices of the *moshav*, the occupant suffered continuous and humiliating challenges from members of the opposite group. Positions occupied by villagers therefore greatly depreciated in value and prestige.

In Ritual

The sphere of ritual was another arena in which the competition between *hamulot* was manifested, materially and otherwise. Since they settled in Romema, the Bitons have acquired two Torah scrolls,[2] each costing about IL. 2,000 ($600). On their arrival in Romema they had had no scrolls, while the Sebags owned two, which they had inherited. Later on, the Sebags acquired two new scrolls. During a lecture by the regional rabbi, he suggested, politely but firmly, that the Romemites should put an end to the acquisition of new Torah scrolls. He made it clear that there were more than enough scrolls in Romema and that such acquisitions

[2] The Torah scrolls are indispensable for the maintenance of religious services. Only minor prayers on some of the weekdays do not require public reading from the Torah. See Deshen 1970:110–111, also Chapter 8:219–220.

appeared, unfortunately, to be motivated by personal pride rather than by genuine concern for religious needs.

The Sebags and the Bitons also competed in the synagogue over large contributions toward various religious purposes and charities. The competition was particularly fierce in the practice of the "selling of *mitzvot*," an activity whereby the worshiper acquires the privilege of being called up to the Torah during the ritual by contributing to the synagogue funds. A portion of the Torah is read on every Sabbath and festival and is recited by a special reader (a *ba'al koreh*); the worshiper who has been called up pronounces benedictions before and after the reading. The act of being called up to the Torah is termed *aliyah* (pl. *aliyot*), meaning "going up." Since the privilege to fulfill the obligation of reading from the Torah cannot be bestowed on every male worshiper [3] the same day (there are only seven *aliyot* on the Sabbath), *aliyot* are sold to the "highest bidder." The act of "selling *aliyot*" is called *mekhirat aliyot* or *mekhirat mitzvot*. (This method of raising funds, but not necessarily the competitive aspect, is common to many synagogues.)

A New Style of Behavior in Ritual
Behavior at Home

Different patterns of behavior between the groups were developing in various spheres of life. Of particular importance was a varying approach to women's work on the farms. In Amran, women had not performed any economic activi-

---

[3] The devout consider it desirable that every male worshiper over thirteen (after his *bar mitzvah*, a rite that initiates him into the full observance of the laws) have an *aliyah*, which is simultaneously an obligation and a privilege, at least once a month. A worshiper who commemorates the death of a relative is usually honored with an *aliyah*.

ties outside the home. This exclusion of women from work beyond the family fold barred them in effect from the company of unrelated men and was strongly supported by religious sanctions. Farming in Israel, however, created pressures and incentives to let women participate in outdoor economic activities. The participation of women in farming both sustained the expansion in the scale of farming and obviated the need for, and the expense of, hired labor. While most of the women among the Sebags were regular daily workers on either their own farms or those of relatives, most of the Biton women were only occasional workers. Thus the Bitons, who forbade their women to work regularly, adhered more strictly to traditional norms of morality and thus forwent certain material advantages. This is in contrast to the Sebags, who encouraged—indeed some of them even forced—their women to help them in their economic enterprises. These different modes of behavior toward women working seem to be closely congruous with the development of different styles of behavior in ritual.[4]

Behavior at Synagogue

The development in ritual of a new style of behavior, which affected the modes of competition in Romema, received dramatic expression in the middle of 1965 when the Bitons withdrew from the synagogue of the community and established a new one which was called the "Biton's Synagogue." Until then all the settlers had prayed in one communal house of worship (as they had in Morocco), which had been built specifically for this purpose by the settlement authorities and the Ministry of Religious Affairs. The core of

[4] For more details about women's work in Romema, see Shokeid 1971a, 1971b.

the Biton group left the communal synagogue because of an issue which developed into a serious dispute. A Biton had been refused the privilege of reading the *haftarah* [5] (an honored part of the ritual) on the last day of Passover unless he paid for it. Since that day happened also to be the anniversary of his grandfather's death, he had expected to have the privilege extended to him without payment.

The new synagogue was housed in a small shed, built for that purpose in the yard of David Biton—one of the more learned Bitons—who became the leader of the new congregation. The new synagogue seemed to be very different from the communal one both in its physical surroundings and in the atmosphere and procedure of ritual. In comparison with the impressive communal house of prayer which was built and supported by public funds, the Biton synagogue was a modest structure. It was very crowded when in use, and the children were not allowed to run about and make noise. But neither were the children permitted to take part in leading some of the prayers (as is the custom in Moroccan synagogues), a practice which frequently caused disorder in the communal synagogue. During the service it was quieter than in the larger communal synagogue, which had both a bigger area and more congregants. People did not talk; if anyone did, David, the leader of the congregation, immediately silenced him. The Bitons' decision not to "sell *mitzvot*" in their congregation was of major significance. They regarded this custom as morally wrong, since it prevented the poor from participating in certain parts of the ritual and because, they argued, it brought into play materialistic elements that they considered unsuited to religious devotion. Instead, David

[5] The *haftarah* is a portion from a book of the Prophets read after the reading of the Torah.

distributed the honors among the congregants. Contributions to the Biton synagogue were voluntary. Quite frequently, congregants told David at the end of the Sabbath prayers that they wished to contribute some money. Such contributions were usually not divulged publicly. As a result, ritual proceedings at the Bitons' synagogue were marked by relative simplicity, modesty, and discipline. The Bitons claimed with pride that in their congregation an atmosphere of sincere religious devotion reigned that sharply contrasted with the "unholy" tone of the communal congregation. They consequently considered themselves morally superior to the communal congregation, which, since they had left it, was dominated by the Sebags. The latter, on the other hand, proved their piety and devotion through monetary generosity, giving large donations at the "selling of *mitzvot*," as well as to the poor scholars or representatives of religious institutions who visited Romema. But there was, of course, no objective criterion by which moral superiority could be accorded to either of the groups. Outsiders (visitors, *moshav* officers, and other officials) praised the Bitons for the order during prayers and the Sebags for their generosity.

The rabbi of Romema, who was an outsider to the community, had no easy life as the religious leader of Romema. His position was seriously undermined both by the turmoil in the large congregation and by the Bitons' secession. He was therefore very ambivalent toward both groups. He used to state that the Sebags were certainly generous, but he argued that their generosity was not "for the sake of God" (*lo leshem shamayim*) but for the sake of their earthly pride. He bitterly criticized their behavior in the synagogue, which often led to fierce arguments and quarrels that disturbed the proceedings of the ritual. As for the Bitons, he attributed their leaving to their quarrelsome nature and to their envy of the Sebags rather than to any spiritual aims. Nevertheless, in order to retain his apparent neutrality and some standing as the rabbi of the community, he prayed from time to time in the Biton congregation, thereby confirming that the Bitons also properly managed their own ritual affairs.

I also observed different patterns of behavior in particular ceremonies, including those which took place outside the synagogue. In those ceremonies, one of which will be described in the following section, the Bitons again demonstrated modesty, simplicity, austere traditional behavior, and an attitude of equality toward all men. The Sebags, who behaved with congenial conviviality, performed their religious duties with an air of opulence and unrestrained generosity.

Behavior at Pilgrimage Festivities

The first week in May 1966 was a very busy one in Romema. Gatherings for prayers and meals in honor of Rabbi Meir Ba'al Ha'Ness were held in various homes on most evenings. Meir Ba'al Ha'Ness, believed by many to be a distinguished scholar and saint who lived in the second century and is thought to be buried in Tiberias, on the Lake of Galilee, is one of the most popular figures in Oriental Jewish tradition. The annual celebrations held at his tomb in Tiberias on the 14th of Iyar (in 1966 the Jewish date fell on May 4) start off a week of festivities culminating in the memorial day of Rabbi Shimeon bar Yohai, on the 18th of Iyar. Lag Ba'Omer, a Jewish festival that ends thirty-three days of ritual mourning during which, among other restrictions, the faithful do not cut their hair and marriages are not performed, falls on the same day. Rabbi Shimeon bar Yohai is probably the most important post-biblical figure in Jewish folk tradition. Historical records substantiate the belief that he lived during the second century and was famous as a scholar and a patriot who opposed the Romans' occupation of Israel. Legend has it that during his flight from the Romans he spent thirteen years, together with his son Eleazar, in a cave in the mountains of Galilee. Meron, a village on a hill near the town of Safed, was the center of his activities and is the site where he and his son are buried. Tradition ascribes to him the writing of the *Zohar* (see p. 43).

The 18th of Iyar is a day of joy and celebration, and religious Jews throng to Meron to pray at the tomb of Rabbi Shimeon bar Yohai. His memory is a source of inspiration and joy to the pious and of hope to those who suffer from all sorts of misfortunes. It is said that the sick may be healed by visiting his tomb. Boys are brought to Meron for their first haircut; their hair is later burned in the fire which is kindled on a pillar on the roof of the tomb. Into the same fire people throw personal belongings, such as scarfs and handkerchiefs, or candles, to help feed the fire; hoping for good luck by this act of devotion. Money and candles are thrown on the tomb itself which are later used for charity or religious purposes.

Around the middle of April, Levy Biton suggested to me that we go to Meron in my car, on Lag Ba'Omer. One of the wealthier farmers in Romema, Levy Biton owned a tractor and was also employed as a village guard. He was a member of the village committee and a leader of the Biton group. Economically and politically he was undoubtedly one of the most powerful persons in Romema. Levy told me that he went on pilgrimage to Meron annually. Two years previously, on Lag Ba'Omer, he had been persuaded to stay at home in order to sow cucumbers. While working with his tractor he carelessly damaged a part which cost him IL. 250 (approximately $70) to repair, and as if that was not enough, the electric battery suddenly broke down the following day. The damage came to about IL. 700 altogether (approximately $200), and since then he has made it a rule to go to Meron every year on Lag Ba'Omer.

Levy suggested that we leave at midnight on the 17th of Iyar in order to arrive in Meron toward morning and be able to spend the whole day of Lag Ba'Omer and that night there. He bought a goat and slaughtered it, giving half to his old father who was not expected to travel; the other half was prepared by his wife and mother to be taken to Meron. Our party eventually came to include Levy, his brother Yoash, and his mother. Levy's wife stayed behind to look after their many small children. His mother, who was glad of the opportunity to go to Meron, was expected to cook for the men. (During his wife's absence Levy's father was looked after by a young unmarried daughter.) At 2 A.M., the night before Lag Ba'Omer, we left Romema for Meron loaded with food, cooking utensils, oil, crockery, and blankets.

Another group of Romemites, members of the Sebag family, was also preparing to leave for Meron. This party included Aziz Sebag, the eldest son of the former head of Amran, his mother, his paternal cousin Yoram and his wife, his paternal uncle who was also his father-in-law, and his mother-in-law. Aziz's own wife stayed behind to look after the children. The Sebags went to Meron in a van which they had hired for about IL. 230 ($65). A few others, including one young couple, went independently to Meron or together with relatives from other parts of the country. The scene, however, was dominated by the two expeditions just described, which were being prepared in advance and avidly discussed in Romema.

When we arrived at the bottom of the hill of Meron, at 8 A.M., an enormous, colorful, and festive crowd had already gathered. Meron, one of the most beautiful spots in Galilee, on this lovely day was bathed in sunlight. The hill, spotted with countless colorful tents, played host to the gaiest assemblage I had ever beheld in Israel—the holy site seemed like a merry fair. Parking the car, we made our way through the long line of pilgrims toward the summit of the hill where the tomb was. We carried our luggage, as did all the others, and Levy's mother joined the women in ululating, thereby expressing not only her own excitement but that of the whole group. At every step we noticed people happily meeting acquaintances from all parts of the country. Others were putting up tents, cooking food, slaughtering animals, dancing, and singing. Levy was leading us toward the top of the hill, passing through the courtyard of Rabbi Shimeon's tomb. Eventually we stopped at a quiet corner, a secluded spot near a wall and a tree which gave some shade and privacy. The place was cut off from the stream of pilgrims pressing forward toward the tomb. We spread our provisions on the ground at that remote spot and began preparing for breakfast. Although we assumed that only we would occupy the spot, we were soon approached by newcomers who wanted to share it with us. Levy declared that in Meron everybody should be welcome, and he invited the newcomers, who were also of Moroccan origin, to share our breakfast.

After breakfast, Levy's mother stayed behind while the three of us went for a walk to the tomb. We bought some candles, and then we pushed our way through the walled courtyard into the densely crowded hall which housed the tomb. Like the other pilgrims, we threw candles on the tomb. We then went out, visiting some of the many caves in the area where scholars are believed to have lived and been buried in ancient times. Along the way Levy gave alms to the beggars who hovered not only near the gates of the tomb but also at the entrance of the caves. Strolling leisurely, we met and greeted relatives and friends of the Romemites, gossiping and exchanging information about others who had either been met in Meron or were not expected to come.

We then came across Aziz Sebag's group. They had put up a tent in the very center of the most crowded area surrounding the tomb. Levy commented that our spot was better since we enjoyed the shade of a wall and a tree and therefore would escape the heat of the burning sun at noon. That comment, however, revealed Levy's awareness that Aziz, by putting up a tent in the center of Meron, had established his group in a grand manner. As we reached the Sebags, they were preparing a goat brought from Romema for slaughter on the spot by a qualified slaughterer, a member of the Mahluf group who had left Romema for a village near Meron a few years earlier. Meat slaughtered at Meron is more meritorious than meat brought to Meron already prepared.

After conversing with the Sebags for a while, we continued our stroll, from time to time returning to our own spot to rest, to eat, or to have some tea. We stopped to talk with newcomers and to watch or join groups of people dancing and singing. The Romemites were continually bumping into acquaintances and happily greeting and chatting with even complete strangers of Moroccan origin. The scene seemed to be dominated by two main distinctive groups: Moroccan Jews and ultra-Orthodox European Jews (Ashkenazim).[6] The Moroccan Jews, the largest single ethnic group gathered in Meron, form also one of the biggest communities of "Oriental"[7] Jews in Israel. Generally, the Moroccan is distinguished by his darker facial features. The older Moroccans of rural origin still wear the *djelaba*, a long, either white or brown gown. Most of them, particularly those of rural origin, speak mainly Mughrabi, the particular Arabic dialect of Moroccan Jews.

The ultra-Orthodox Ashkenazim, most of whom crowded the courtyard and the buildings of the tomb, being in charge of the site, seemed to dominate the place. They could be distinguished by sidelocks and a beard, the dress of Orthodox eastern European Jews which consists of a long black coat (*kapota*) and a particular hat trimmed with fur (a *shtreimel*), and the use of Yiddish as the language for daily intercourse.

In the afternoon, we observed what was going on in the front court of the tomb from the vantage spot of a balcony. Below, the court, a walled enclosure, was packed with people on their way to the tomb or loitering in order to exchange greetings or to give alms to mendicants and contributions to solicitors for various charity funds and religious institutions. They were waiting around to be blessed by the representatives of institutions and charities who were at the court. Most of the rabbis and the solicitors for charity were of Ashkenazi extraction.

Watching the busy crowd at the court for a while, Levy

[6] *Ashkenazi*, variant of Jewish tradition and custom that developed in medieval central and northern Europe, also used when referring to adherents thereof.

[7] The term "Oriental Jews" is used in Israel to denote immigrants from Middle Eastern and North African countries, while "Western Jews" and Ashkenazim are terms used to denote immigrants from northern Europe and America.

suddenly spotted Aziz Sebag, who looked smart and happy in his new clothes (which he had donned since we had met him that morning) and was sporting an attractive embroidered velvet skullcap. He was greeting acquaintances and other people in the crowd, mainly the Ashkenazi Jews who were in charge of the place and conducted its main ceremonies, offering them drinks from the bottle of brandy in his hand and exchanging kisses on the cheek. He seemed to be enjoying the atmosphere of generosity and brotherhood which prevailed among all the pilgrims to Meron. We soon also espied Yoram Sebag and his wife. They were smartly dressed and, like Aziz, Yoram held a bottle of brandy and was offering drinks; his wife was holding the glasses. In the meantime, Aziz and his group noticed us looking down and greeted us joyfully. We stayed on the balcony for a few minutes longer and then left for dinner.

After dinner, Levy decided that it was now time to distribute drinks and meat at the tomb as they had done every year. He took a bottle of wine and a bottle of arak (a traditional oriental alcoholic drink which is now often replaced by brandy), from which we had already drunk during dinner, and Levy's mother took a bag of sliced cooked meat. Levy, who walked at the head of our group, told me on the way about the Lag Ba'Omer custom in Morocco to exchange food and to give certain parts of the slaughtered animal to the poor.

It was already dark when we arrived at the back entrance of the tomb. Levy had decided to distribute his food and drinks to the beggars and other pathetic characters sitting along the outside walls of the tomb, particularly near the back door, expecting contributions from the people leaving the shrine. We also offered food to the visitors who were leaving the tomb. Yoash held the bottles, Levy offered glasses of wine or arak, and their mother handed out meat. The Bitons behaved as though they were performing a duty and the entire group showed no sign of either gaiety or pleasure as had been manifested earlier by the Sebags. Levy, however, told me how pleased he was that his efforts at distributing the food were succeeding, for people even approached him and asked for drinks. Yet his efforts could not dispel the sense of misery that dominated the scene, generated by the beggars and other unfortunates, as well as by the dirt which had accumulated at the end of this busy day in the backyard of the tomb. Yoash must have noticed how wretched the whole atmosphere was because he suddenly told me (while his brother and mother were still busy at their tasks) that he disapproved of discriminating between one Jew and another. He implied that he liked sharing their food with all Jews, particularly with the miserable, poor, and unimportant. I have no doubt that Yoash was implicitly comparing our group with the Sebags', whom we had observed earlier at the center of the festivities. The Sebags had shared drinks and exchanged greetings and kisses with the Ashkenazim, who formed the elite group of Meron. While the Sebags had been smartly dressed and had approached the more prosperous persons as equals at this ceremony, the Bitons, without changing their clothes, went out at twilight and approached those at the back door who were certain to accept their offerings. It was unimaginable that the beggars would refuse the food and drink.

At about 9 P.M. we were ready to turn in, but Levy now realized that it was too cold to spend the night at the spot we had selected, since there was no proper shelter and the place was open to the wind. We therefore began to look for a place

to camp somewhere down the hill. We found an abandoned
fire which we relit to warm ourselves. Sitting around the
fire, relishing its warmth, we were approached by an old,
impressive-looking Ashkenazi Jew who asked us humbly
whether he might join us and warm himself. He was wearing
a *kapota* and a *shtreimel* and carried a black briefcase. His
white face, which was dominated by his childlike blue eyes,
was graced by a long beard. Levy welcomed him heartily
and offered him food and drink. But our guest politely refused and asked instead for bread and water.[8]

Through the few remarks and questions addressed to me I
realized that our visitor was a man of learning who possessed
a wide general knowledge and who had a deep insight into
human nature. Among other things, he had survived the
Nazi Holocaust. He entertained us with commentaries on
the Torah and related to us stories and anecdotes about the
behavior of ancient scholars. It was obvious that he kept his
talk at his hosts' level of knowledge. His audience by now included one more Moroccan who had also been welcomed by
Levy and had been offered food. Like Levy and Yoash, the
newcomer treated the Ashkenazi guest with much respect
and asked him various questions about the Torah and Jewish
history, such as, "How much time has elapsed since the
Israelite Exodus from Egypt?" Although some of the questions were quite naïve, he answered them seriously and
kindly. Nobody asked our guest any personal questions,[9]

[8] I assume that he suspected that the rules of *kashrut* (ritual preparation
of food) were not scrupulously observed.

[9] I tried, once, in a delicate manner, to identify some of his social background, but he avoided any direct answer. I did not pursue the matter,
since I did not want to disturb the natural course of affairs. He seemed to
be quite curious about my own involvement with the Romemites. We both

and when he got up to leave, Levy asked for his blessing. As he fulfilled this request, Levy gave him some money, which he did not refuse. I assume it was a banknote of either IL. 5 or IL. 10—approximately $1.50 or $3.00.

After his departure, Levy told me that he was glad of the meeting with the Ashkenazi and that there had been a similar meeting last year when a Yemenite scholar had blessed them. I suspect that Levy associated these meetings with the supernatural. It was as if these persons, accepted as everyday types on other occasions, suddenly became messengers of fate, appearing as they did in Meron on Lag Ba'Omer. It was a fortuitous and gratifying end to a holy day, characterized by brotherhood and generosity.

We spent a bitterly cold night, hardly sleeping, and left early in the morning for home, paying another short visit to the tomb and to some of the caves before our departure. On our way home we passed through Haifa and made a short stop at a cave known as "Elijah's cave," where, according to folk tradition, the prophet Elijah stayed for some time. After breakfasting there, we continued on our journey, arriving in Romema before noon. The Sebags did not go straight home from Meron, but went on a further pilgrimage to the tomb of Rabbi Meir Ba'al Ha'Ness at Tiberias. They arrived in Romema late at night.

The Functions of Pilgrimage

I turn to analyze the Romemites' behavior at Meron, its implications, and latent functions on two levels: First I shall look at the behavior of both groups of pilgrims, the Bitons and the Sebags, as one phenomenon; second, I shall differen-

---

were in a similar position in that it was difficult for either of us to talk freely about ourselves.

tiate between the Bitons' behavior and that of the Sebags in the same ceremonial context.

Behavior of Both Groups as a Single Phenomenon

The following facts should be noted: On this occasion the Romemites as a whole had the opportunity to meet relatives, friends, and acquaintances (from Amran and from other parts of Morocco now living in various locations in Israel), many of whom they had not seen for years either before or after migration. In addition, information was also exchanged about many who had not come to Meron. The conversations touched on various spheres of life, such as personal, social, technical, geographic, and professional. People were acquainting one another with what had happened to them and to others since last they had met. It was an opportunity to show off achievements, to share good fortune, and to express sympathy for misfortunes. At the same time it was an occasion for making new acquaintances and friends. In a sense it was a ceremony of social reintegration of the former Amranites as well as of the Moroccan community at large.

The "ingathering of the Moroccan community" was, however, only one of the latent functions of the pilgrimage to Meron. The Romemites in Meron also had the opportunity to meet and interact on equal terms with other sectors of Israeli society. The coming together of the traditional Moroccans and the Orthodox Ashkenazim was in many ways a confrontation between two polar sectors of Israeli society. Although both sectors are equally devoted to traditional Judaism, they differ in the performance of rituals and rites, as well as in other personal and social spheres.

Arriving as a distinctive large group, the Moroccans counterbalanced the smaller but dominant Ashkenazi group in

Meron. Moroccans and Ashkenazim, as well as other ethnic groups, intermingled and confronted one another on apparently equal terms. In an atmosphere dominated by ancient common beliefs, gaiety, and generosity, social and cultural barriers were removed. I refer here to the festive and congenial atmosphere which prevailed when the Sebags and the Ashkenazim mingled in the courtyard of the tomb as well as to the mutual sympathy and respect shown by the Bitons and the Ashkenazi around the fire.

The general relaxation of the Romemites in their interpersonal relationships was significant: their friendliness at Meron contrasted with their quarrelsomeness in Romema. At home the leaders of the two groups, Aziz Sebag and Levy Biton, were bitter opponents maliciously expressing their mutual dislike. Only recently Levy had manipulated public opinion to demand Aziz's removal from land which was not his own but which he had already sown. Nevertheless, in Meron they were courteous and even friendly to one another. Yoash, Levy's brother, although an amiable person, always supported his brother's uncompromising opinions of other people and rigid attitude toward village policies. Now, however, he was extremely kind to everybody, including Aziz. Without any apparent reason he told me that he and his father had a "white heart" (lev lavan) and that neither bore a grudge. Thus he separated himself from his brother, who was a bitter foe of his opponents. He said that he regretted his recent rage at Aziz during the dispute over the latter's expansion in farming. In the meantime he had realized that there were more people in Romema, as well as in other villages, who behaved in the same way. Therefore it was not fair to attack and blame only one person.

The analysis of the behavior of all the Romema pilgrims as

representing one phenomenon is in line with the structural-functional approach to the analysis of rites and ceremonies, which demonstrates the contribution of the ceremonial to the integration and solidarity of society (Malinowski 1948:33, 35; Radcliffe-Brown 1952:149, 152). Thus, the pilgrimage of the Romemites on Lag Ba'Omer to Meron: (1) served to integrate the Moroccans into the wider context of the Israeli Jewish society in which Moroccans and Ashkenazim (including religious as well as nonreligious Ashkenazim) frequently appear as separate social and cultural groups; (2) seemed to contribute to the reunion of the dispersed Moroccan community in Israel; (3) seemed to effect at least a temporary "cease-fire" within the smaller context of the Romemite community and to permit some affective relationship among the Romemites themselves who were regularly involved in bitter internal disputes.

Differential Behavior of the Two Groups

From the early stages of planning the trip to Meron, the Bitons behaved differently from the Sebags. Although Levy was probably more prosperous than Aziz (though the Sebag company also included Yoram, who, compared to Levy's brother, was well off), the Sebag group planned and staged a much more opulent celebration. The Sebags' preparations were a topic of lively conversation in Romema and were bound to impress the people they met in Meron, both Romemites and others. Arriving in Meron, bringing a live goat to be slaughtered on the spot, the Sebags pitched a tent made of blankets, carpets, and poles at a most strategic point, facing the main stream of visitors, who had to pass them on their way to and from the tomb. They therefore had the opportunity to meet and be seen by as many as possible of their acquaintances who had come to Meron. Levy's party, on the other hand, established itself in a very remote corner where they could meet or be met by their acquaintances only if they left their camp to walk around the area. But the main difference between the two parties was highlighted in their respective manner of acting as hosts to strangers and distributing food and drinks. The Sebags changed into their best clothes and approached the elite group among the congregants in Meron at the central spot of the celebrations, in the daytime. The Bitons showed their hospitality at the back entrance to the shrine, choosing surroundings which were shabby in environment and in audience. According to their own claim, they intended to perform a *mitzvah* (a religious precept) of sharing their food with the poor. The end of the day which brought along the strange Ashkenazi scholar was in a way proof to the Bitons that their pilgrimage had been well received. They were thus generously rewarded both in social and religious terms.

There is no doubt that religious motives and expectations as well as the striving for social recognition and approval for secular achievements (social and material) in part motivated the behavior of both the Bitons and the Sebags in Meron. Both groups, originating from the same cultural background, were striving for the same goals—piety and social recognition. Our observations nevertheless revealed a difference in style of behavior: the Sebags' efforts were concentrated in a display of extravagance, appealing to new social groups, while throughout the ceremony the Bitons were materially and socially humble in their performance. It is my intention to stress that the pilgrimage to Meron provided each group with the opportunity to claim, to express, and to stabilize its own separate social and moral self-image, already emerging in the contrasting styles of the two synagogues in Romema. Thus the same situation which generates intracommunal solidarity and relaxation also provides the participants with a welcomed possibility to express and even stress their social differentiation.

A Breakthrough in the System of Equalizing Gains

Following Gluckman's presentation (1962:14–15) that ceremonial can profitably be analyzed in terms of social relationships, I think that the differences in behavior which I observed in Meron can better be understood when analyzed within the full complex of the Romemites' relationships and behavior in other spheres of life. I mentioned earlier the continuing competition in Romema between the two family groups, of which the two parties of pilgrims formed a part. The social and economic differentiation that had existed between them in Morocco had greatly changed in Israel. In occupation, economic resources, and in political positions and rights, the Bitons had reached a level of equality and opportunity with the previously wealthier Sebags. Yet both groups were striving for differential status and therefore continuously competed for prestige in various spheres of life both within and outside of their community. Since the linear competition in economics, politics, and ritual frequently enabled both parties to equalize their gains either by struggling for the same achievements or by preventing any gains to be had by any of the competitors, these patterns of competition generated an endless process of equalizing gains and maintained thereby a permanent uncertainty over the differentiation of status. In order to achieve a permanent gain in their competition, they had to break through the system of equalizing gains, which could be done only by a completely new strategy, or by evolving new rules or new spheres of competition. Thus, according to my analysis, instead of trying "to be the same," some of the Romemites (the Bitons in the first stage) reversed their efforts and tried "to be different," at least in some aspects of ritual. I defined those modes of differences in behavior as differences in style only, since they do not entail a rejection of the basic values and symbols related to the sphere under change. Such a mode of behavior involves a special selection and emphasis of particular norms and symbols and their reinterpretation among the vast and sometimes ambiguous pool of cultural and religious precepts. I assume that under certain conditions a new style may develop a completely new body of beliefs and code of normative behavior. Thus, for example, the antagonism raised by a new style among the Orthodox community and hierarchy may be a factor in such a development.

Flexibility of meaning and interpretation of symbols and norms seems to be an important feature of the ritual domain, akin to the flexibility of legal concepts which Gluckman observed and analyzed (1955). It appears as if flexibility is inherent in the legal system and probably even more so in universal religious systems, which control normative and moral behavior of individuals and groups maintaining various personal statuses, different social positions, and socioeconomic standing in society through continuously changing circumstances. A religious system which caters, for example, to both the poor and the rich, the ignorant and the educated, must provide various justifications and stimuli to its different adherents. Therefore, the religious domain seems to be particularly suitable for developing differences within apparently homogeneous and centralized groups and nations.

The sphere of ritual provided an almost unique opportunity to the Romemites for a breakthrough in the "vicious" circle of equalizing gains since it offered the necessary ideological legitimation for a new way to measure gains. The different styles of both groups were rooted in Jewish tradition. The vast body of Jewish religious literature provides different and what at times would seem to be even contradictory interpretations of the ideal mode of behavior in man's relationship to God and his relationships to his fellowmen. Jewish tradition also has different scales for evaluating man's conditions of daily existence. Thus, for example, while some early normative sources praise the poor and the modest for their moral superiority in their daily life and in religious behavior, others commend generosity and the man who worships God in splendor. Thus the actions of the Bitons, who tried "to be different" by adopting a style of modesty which emphasized equality among men and traditional morality, had their legitimate basis in religious mores as much as the Sebags' style of generosity, impressive donations, and lavish manner of worship. While the Sebags viewed their opulent behavior as a rejoicing in and worshiping of God with grace, the Bitons denounced this conduct as ostentatious: the Bitons saw themselves as austere and genuinely benevolent to the poor and miserable, whereas the Sebags considered their behavior mean and miserly.

The fabric of the new competition was observed at the proceedings of ritual at the Bitons' synagogue. Yet the establishment of the synagogue was an act of physical separation generated apparently by a single, overt, personal dispute. The phenomenon was also observed in Meron, on neutral ground, where both groups watched each other amicably and expressed their rivalry in peaceful but striking terms and not in the context of dispute and separation which prevailed in their territory (Shokeid 1971b). It was probably easier for the Sebags to choose extravagance and for the Bitons to opt for modesty, since in the past the Sebags had experienced more affluence than the Bitons. At the same time, however, there seem to be some strains intrinsic to the situation which compelled the two parties to adopt those contrasting styles both in familiar surroundings (Romema) and on strange grounds (Meron). In both cases they were observed by other former Amranites (settlers of Romema and other places), as well as by other people acquainted with the Amranites' past stratification. The Sebags were driven to maintain an opulent style in order to assert that they had not come down in the world. I maintain that the Bitons, behaving in an ascetic, unostentatious style, asserted that though they had attained a better economic position, they had not adopted pretentious modes of behavior. Had the Bitons behaved opulently, they would have appeared as *nouveau riche*, pretending beyond their original station.[10] The development of different norms of behavior in spheres of life closely connected with tradition and religion, such as norms relating to women's roles, underwrote the two groups' distinct behavior—opulence versus moderation—with a wider and deeper divergence in values and ways of life.

Boissevain's description of the competition at fiestas [11] held in Maltese villages (1969) has made an important contribution to the study of behavior at ritual. Maltese villages were often divided into two groups (*partiti*) of worshipers of different saints. This division, which occurred during the lat-

---

[10] See for example Colson's description (1953) of denouncements of *nouveau riche* pretensions in a previously strictly stratified society.

[11] In Malta the term is *festa*.

ter half of the nineteen century, when there were drastic economic and social developments throughout Malta, was manifested on various occasions in competition and dispute: it was regularly and strongly expressed at the annual fiesta for each saint. During these fiestas each group of worshipers tried to outdo the other in the grandeur of its celebrations.[12] Except for some highly tentative suggestions, however, Boissevain did not identify precisely the principles and motives underlying the *partiti* affiliation, and in this respect his analysis of the phenomenon of competition at fiestas is not fully developed.

Boissevain suggested, however, that choosing a different saint for worship might have been a form of protest by a particular group against the established authority. This choice of protest, whatever its origins, was legitimate within the framework of Maltese values and norms and established the particular form of competition between *partiti*, which led to a process of equalizing gains. In this competition the sides hardly ever make a safe and permanent gain vis-à-vis the others. Even though the participants' claims for differential status were not confirmed through the ritual, the *partiti* nevertheless became a vehicle through which Maltese traditional symbols were affirmed. The Romemites, on the other hand, whose political behavior was to a large extent similar to that of the Maltese in *partiti* competition, made a choice which ended the process of equalizing gains, at least in the sphere of

---

[12] "The *partiti* compete over almost every aspect of the *fiesta*, including the decoration of the streets, the adornment of the statue, the number of guest bands, and above all, the fireworks. Even the exact number of communicants, the size of candles and the quantity of light bulbs illuminating the facade of the church often become the subject of dispute" (Boissevain 1969:75).

ritual. At the same time they also affirmed traditional Jewish norms.

For my purposes, the information about the fiesta and its social framework is too limited to pursue the comparison. It remains for further research and analysis to see under what social and cultural circumstances people turn to a choice which leads toward a competition of continued equalizing gains, and under what conditions they choose a new style which leads toward a sort of equilibrium. The latter situation may be a basis for observing and analyzing the development of new movements and sects, particularly those with more ascetic orientations, within the folds of established religions. Thus it seems possible to advance hypotheses about the behavior of groups which have recently attained economic prosperity and social importance but which are still competing for social esteem with the traditionally established groups. Since the traditional elite groups may be better versed and more adept in etiquette and have better access to more paraphernalia of prestige pertaining to various spheres of life, including the religious, the new ambitious groups may choose one of two main alternatives: (a) either to compete for prestige in the various relevant domains by a process inducing equalizing gains (thereby incurring the epithet of *nouveau riche* behavior); or (b) at some time to try to establish a new style of behavior and new critieria for measuring prestige. The religious domain in particular, because of its flexibility, seems to provide congenial conditions and opportunities for such a development. I suggest, although hesitantly, since I did not pursue the subject, that the above hypothesis be used in pursuing the development of ascetic Protestantism.

Jewish religion and its world community also went through a process of sectarianism such as, for example, the development of the Hasidic movement and its various branches since the eighteenth century (Katz 1961). But contrary to parallel developments in Christianity and Islam, rarely did sectarian movements lead to a formal split in Judaism and in the Jewish community. This probably was due primarily to the fact that since the destruction of the Temple the Jewish community and its religious leaders have not been centralized by any official ecclesiastical hierarchy.[13] Second, religious division in Judaism had no political consequences and could not find expression in secular power, as did, for example, certain Islamic ascetic movements (see Evans-Pritchard 1949). However, some of the innovating movements and groups within Judaism might also have developed through the process suggested here.

[13] The establishment of the office of the chief rabbinate in Israel may change the pattern of a noncentralized religion.

CHAPTER 3

The Memorial Celebrations of Tunisian Immigrants

SHLOMO DESHEN

Cultural ethnic activities in Israel have become increasingly popular since the early 1960s. Immigrants from specific regions or countries have organized associations which are active in many cultural fields. These publish material relating to their particular religiocultural heritage and they renew traditional festivities which had been popular in their countries of origin but were neglected in Israel. During the 1950s, the years of mass immigration to Israel from North Africa, these activities were almost nonexistent.

This chapter deals with the phenomenological nature of the increasing popularity of *hillulot* (sing. *hillula*), memorial celebrations of Tunisian immigrants. I broach questions such as: Why do the actors participate in these memorial celebrations? What general sociocultural processes can be discerned operating in them? What kind of existential situation do the actors express through their participation?

The first section outlines Jewish Tunisian memorial rites in general and describes Tunisian immigrants in Israel. The second depicts two *hillulot* that I observed. In the third section I discuss the implications of the data.

Tunisian Jews in Israel
Cultural Background—Memorial Rites

Judeo-Tunisian memorial rites, rooted in the particular theology of Kabalism, initially centered around the demise of pious men whose death was conceived as a mystical marriage of their souls with God; hence the term *hillula* (literally "feast" or "wedding feast") for memorial rites. To Kabalists the commemoration of the death of a mystic was an auspicious time, during which secrets of the holy texts might be revealed. The memorial day of mystics came to be marked by study, meditation, and prayer.

In time memorial rites also came to be held in honor of persons who had not been saintly mystics but were accorded respect because of kinship or other ties. In popular sentiment and custom these commemorations became joyful celebrations, and some of them attracted multitudes of pilgrims. In folk practice the idea developed that the commemorated saint would intercede with God on behalf of the worshiper. Many spiritually or physically afflicted persons piously and devotedly make the pilgrimage to the memorial site in the hope of being cured or relieved. While such pilgrimages are made throughout the year, they are most common on the anniversary of death.

These practices, very popular among both rabbis and the common people for generations, have been looked upon with disapproval by many representative figures of the literary tradition whose attitude to this day is ambivalent in the matter. The reason is twofold: (1) theologically, some of the popular beliefs run counter to the strict and austere monotheism of classical Jewish thought; (2) from the practical point of view, the rabbis frowned upon the boisterous atmosphere generated at memorial celebrations. The mingling of men and women in the crowd was objectionable, particularly since it was on hallowed ground—either a synagogue named after a mystic or his graveside—and it took place at so auspicious a time as his memorial day.

Hillulot are not the only means through which the dead are commemorated; the continuing popularity of Tunisian memorial celebrations is manifest in several ways. One practice is to name newly built synagogues after personalities of the Tunisian Jewish past or after other personages whom the congregations wish to honor and whose death they wish to commemorate. Completely new *hillulot*, which focus on Tunisian rabbis who died in Israel in recent years, have also emerged; the most popular are those in honor of Rabbi Hayim Huri, who died in the town of Beersheba in 1957,[1] and of Rabbi Hvita Kohen, who died in the village of Berekhya near Ashkelon in 1958.[2]

Tunisian Immigrants in Israel

About 70,000 Tunisian Jews, either born in Tunisia or of Tunisian extraction, live in Israel. Most of them immigrated in the 1950s and are scattered throughout the country. In some localities they form sizable populations. Their style of life, which had generally been traditional in their country of origin, has greatly changed as a consequence of the social, economic, and cultural circumstances of life in urban, industrialized, dynamic Israel.

Many of these immigrants are beset by a sense of cultural loss, feeling that they have declined in status, specifically

---

[1] For a brief description see Noy 1968:359–361.

[2] For a discussion of the social context of the *hillula* in memory of Rabbi Hvita Kohen see Deshen 1966, 1969b.

religious status. Explicitly, this feeling finds expression (see below, Chapter 6) in nostalgic reminiscence of the respected traditional rabbinical leadership of old. Also, the Tunisian immigrants tend to idealize the Jewish society of the recent past, which they describe as harmonious and pious. This past, wistfully recalled as an old, cherished culture whose reality has become more and more elusive to them, is an important element in the image the immigrants have formed of themselves. While significant, this feeling of decline and loss is not constant in the minds of the Tunisians as a whole in Israel. The feeling varies with different individuals and different groups of Tunisians. How, and how often, it is expressed changes not only with the individuals but with the given situation. Some of the other component factors in the self-image of the Tunisian immigrants are their individual socioeconomic positions and their experience of identifying themselves as Israeli nationals. Later I shall suggest that the underlying reason for the participants' attendance of memorial celebrations might be related to the kind of image they have of themselves.

At first the *hillulot* in Israel were celebrated as personal affairs on a very small scale. Only local people, relatives, and persons who had known the deceased personally attended. In time, however, more and more persons thronged to these *hillulot*, which, in some cases, came to attract thousands from distant localities all over the country. Well-established, as well as new, *hillulot* now take place in many towns and villages that have Tunisian populations, with new ones, focusing on ancient or recently deceased personages, continuing to emerge.[3]

[3] A *hillula* in honor of Rabbi Yehoshua Bessis (Tunis, eighteenth century) was started in Lod in 1970. Another one in honor of Rabbi Matzliah

The phenomenon of the *hillulot* raises such questions as: Why have these activities been resuscitated? What causes their continuing dissemination? These questions cannot be dismissed breezily with the answer that the activities are instances of transplanted traditionalism—first, because the *hillula* activities had not been carried on for a period of about ten years and then were revived and became popular again, and second, because the survival of the traditions of Tunisian Jews (and this could be said of traditions everywhere) has been selective. Why do the *hillulot* survive so vigorously whereas other Tunisian Jewish traditions have sunk into oblivion?

Description of Two *Hillulot*

The very stimulating conception of the nature of religious change presented in the work of Bellah (1964) might afford us an approach to these questions. The symbols and rituals that compose a religion can be categorized on a continuum of their relative differentiation or rationalization. For example, one would categorize the rite of commemoration through the devotional recitation of liturgy by an individual, such as we shall see presently at the *hillulot* festivities, as a religious rite of a relatively rationalized, differentiated, nature. The rite enables the worshiper to confront, as an individual, the existential problem which is motivating his ritual. Individual devotional prayer is a relatively abstract kind of ritual action which allows for individual sentiment and ideas. The decision of an individual to go on pilgrimage is also a religious act of a relatively rationalized nature. On the other hand, participation in memorial rites that are an inherent

Mazuz (murdered in Tunis, early 1971) was started in Pardess Katz in 1971.

part of the routine of social life of one's community would be categorized as an act of a less rationalized nature. So also would be the rite of commemoration through a communal feast, as against individual prayer or individual action of any other ritual kind. Commemoration through a communal feast does not allow for self-abstraction, nor does it encourage the individual to come face to face with his particular and personal existential problems. During communal feasts, moreover, the mystery of the nature of God and the concepts of man, the soul, and death are not confronted as directly and clearly as when a person immerses himself in individual prayer. Thus, despite the fact that the underlying ideas of these two forms of Jewish Tunisian commemoration are the same, there are nuances of difference in the awareness and emphasis of these ideas.

Two *hillulot*, which took place in the town of Ramla (about fifteen miles southeast of Tel Aviv), are described below. One *hillula*, in memory of Rabbi Yosseif Ma'aravi, was celebrated in the synagogue of the immigrants of Gabès (southern Tunisia), in January 1969; the other, in memory of Rabbi Hai Taieb, was held in the nearby synagogue of immigrants from Tunis a few weeks earlier, in December 1968.

Commemorating Rabbi Yosseif Ma'aravi

According to legend, Rabbi Yosseif Ma'aravi belonged to the famous sixteenth-century group of mystics living in Safed, Palestine (Schechter 1908). He is said to have appeared suddenly in southern Tunisia, where he lived out his life. The reputed grave of the rabbi in El-Hama, near the town of Gabès, has been a place of pilgrimage for Tunisian Jewry for a long time (Allouche 1928). Legends of its miracle-working properties are very popular in Tunisian

Jewish folklore, and new tales, rooted in recent events, continue to evolve. The new legends revolve around miracles that took place during the German occupation of Tunisia in World War II and at the time of immigration of most of the Jews of the region to Israel in the 1950s (Noy 1968:122–125, 361–363).[4]

Some of the immigrants to Israel from Gabès and its environs, who have settled in the town of Ramla, have named their synagogue after Rabbi Yosseif Ma'aravi and in recent years have begun to hold a *hillula* on the reputed anniversary of the saint's death. Originally the celebration was quite modest, with only members of the local congregation attending. The annual commemoration has, however, steadily come to attract more and more people from all over Israel. During the last few years the congregation of the Ramla synagogue has annually sent out posters to southern Tunisian synagogues throughout the country, informing them of the

[4] The following tale on the wonder-working grave is current in the last few years:

The Tomb That Moved from El-Hama to Israel

When the state of Israel was established, the great rabbi Yosseif Ma'aravi—may his memory be blessed!—appeared in a dream to the rabbi of El-Hama and said to him:

"If you want to go to Israel, do it, but do not lose a moment on my account. Do not torment yourself on account of me, because I will go after you to the holy land and I will not stay here in a strange land. And when I come near you, I will give you a sign: the waters of the spring next to my tomb will grow cold."

And thus it truly happened. Today, the spring of El-Hama is like all other springs. Thanks to Rabbi Yosseif Ma'aravi—may his memory be blessed!—the Jews of El-Hama have come to Israel and his tomb has moved after them to the holy land. It is unfortunate that no one in Israel knows where the tomb is to be found. Thanks to the great rabbi and sage, the Messiah, son of David, will come soon in his chariot. Amen! (Noy 1968:125; our translation).

forthcoming *hillula* and inviting people to participate. The 1969 celebrations I attended were advertised by posters which mentioned that that year's celebrations were also in honor of the twentieth anniversary of the state of Israel and of the twentieth anniversary of the foundation of the synagogue. When I asked some of the local people on the spot as to why they, and not other immigrants from Gabès, maintained Rabbi Yosseif's *hillula*, I was told a new legend which has evolved in Israel: One of the women of the congregation had had a dream in which the saint appeared to her and commanded that his grave be honored and that the *hillula* be celebrated as in the past. In her dream the woman had told the saint that this was not possible since they were now in Israel and his grave was abroad. To which the saint replied cryptically that henceforth the grave would be among them.[5] When her dream became known, the synagogue committee ordered a stone from the grave in El-Hama to be sent to them. It was built into the foundations of the Holy Ark [6] when the synagogue was renovated and enlarged. Since then, the Ramla Gabèsans have organized the yearly *hillula* on an increasingly lavish scale.

When I arrived at about six o'clock in the afternoon, thousands of pilgrims had already thronged to the synagogue from all over the country and more were still coming. I estimated their number at over three thousand. They came from as far as Safed in the north and Beersheba in the south. The synagogue and its immediate surroundings bustled and buzzed with excitement. The street leading to the synagogue

[5] The theme of the legend is the same as that of the legend reported by Noy; the difference lies in the purported location of the grave.

[6] The large cupboard at the eastern end of the synagogue that contains the Torah scrolls. This is the most hallowed part of a synagogue.

was decorated with colored lamps and banners welcoming the pilgrims to the *hillula*. The traffic was so heavy that policemen were on hand to direct it. Loudspeakers had been placed at different strategic points and at times during the evening were used simultaneously for diverse purposes, creating a deafening din. The atmosphere in the courtyard of the synagogue was one of gaiety, exuberance, and good feeling, with excitement running high. People greeted each other joyfully; they embraced, kissed—some claiming they had not seen each other for twenty years. These highly charged emotional encounters generated much laughter, shouting, and ebullience.

In one corner of the courtyard a platform had been erected and a band, playing Tunisian tunes, accompanied a popular singer of oriental songs who had been brought from Acre in the North. The repertoire of the singer, who was originally from Tunis, included Tunisian-Arab and traditional Jewish Tunisian songs. He sang with a microphone, and an amplifier projected the music to the farthest corner of the courtyard and beyond. The people milled around the band: some spontaneously broke into oriental dance movements; others listened with one ear, or ignored the music altogether. Instead they boisterously exchanged greetings. Food was generously offered and passed around. Another set of amplifiers transmitted the proceedings inside the synagogue.

At about eight o'clock, when the celebration had been going on for a number of hours, the mayor of Ramla arrived and mounted the platform, flanked by dignitaries of the congregation. The singer, acting as master of ceremonies, tried to say a few words of introduction, which were lost in the general confusion and noise. He then handed over the microphone to the mayor. Throughout these proceedings the band had not stopped playing and people had continued to mill about. The exchange between the singer and the mayor thus looked from a distance like a vaudeville pantomime played out against a background of noise. No disrespect was intended toward the distinguished guest, but the note of formality that the organizers had attempted to inject into this atmosphere of exuberance had been wrongly timed. The spirit of the evening was epitomized by the actions of the young man who was to have handed a big bouquet of carnations to the mayor after the latter had finished his speech. As the speakers on the platform hesitated, looking confusedly at the milling noisy crowd, he jumped onto the platform, bouquet in hand. He thrust the flowers into the arms of the startled mayor, grabbed the microphone and shouted: "This is a gift to the mayor in the name of the whole Tunisian community!" He then faltered and began to stutter, but almost immediately regaining his composure, he bellowed into the microphone: "No! no! A gift from all of us! All the ethnic communities (*kol ha'eidot*)! All of the people of Israel are united! May the spirit of the saint bring peace to the whole state!"

Extending the bouquet to the mayor, an official token of respect on behalf of the congregation, should have been a formal act of appreciation. The mayor's speech should have been heard respectfully instead of being drowned out by the noise of the crowd. And the young man, who was to have represented the congregation in a dignified manner, in his excitement not only faltered in his words, but probably did not convey the intended message, nor did he say it at the appropriate moment. The actual presentation of the flowers was, however, expressive of the whole atmosphere of communality, immediacy, and goodwill. Intended as a symbolic act of local ethnic identity, it became a symbolic act of national communion.

I did not observe the proceedings inside the synagogue on this occasion but did so at another *hillula* described below.

Commemorating Rabbi Hai Taieb

In Judeo-Tunisian folklore, Rabbi Hai Taieb is a saint who worked miracles, and during his lifetime he was greatly held in awe (Arditti 1904). In common parlance he is called "Rebee Hai Taieb Lo Met" (literally: "Rabbi Hai Taieb is not dead"). This is a play on the saint's name (the Judeo-Tunisian name "Hai" corresponding to the Hebrew word for "live") that reflects popular sentiment as to his powers to perform miracles. The phrase *"lo met"* is especially emphasized since it reflects the substantive meaning of the saint's name.

The celebration took place in the synagogue of the northern Tunisian community in Ramla, named after Rabbi Hai Taieb. The synagogue is not far from the one named after Rabbi Yosseif Ma'aravi. The street leading to the house of worship was also decorated with colored lamps, and vendors shouted and plied their wares of traditional sweetmeats. This celebration, though it also attracted many people from distant points in Israel, was held on a smaller scale than the *hillula* of Rabbi Yosseif Ma'aravi; only about fifteen hundred people attended.

On this occasion I concentrated on the proceedings inside the synagogue proper. The interior of the synagogue was adorned with many photographs of scenes from the Jewish quarter of Tunis, such as the Great Synagogue and the rabbinical court. The atmosphere was similar to the one I described earlier, but activities were more diversified. Besides people gaily greeting each other, laughing, and embracing, there were also persons engaged in ritual activities (described below). One of the synagogue beadles was seated near the Holy Ark, a box of wicks on his knees, selling them to all comers. The custom to kindle memorial lights on the anniversary of the dead is a central rite at *hillulot*. People were pressing around the beadle trying to buy a wick so that they could light it in one of the oil containers that hung along the wall near the Ark. In the women's section wicks were also being sold. Each woman placed her wick in a large basin of oil and lit it.

Despite the din created by the milling mass of people and the selling of wicks, many of the men in the crowd near the Ark, especially those in their thirties and early forties, were devoutly reciting the customary memorial texts. The elders, on the other hand, seemed to be concentrated at the other end of the synagogue, seated around a table laden with food and drink, partaking of the ceremonial meal which is also a central feature of memorial rites. There was a marked contrast between the expressions of devotion of the men around the Ark and those seated around the feasting table and elsewhere in the synagogue. One young man in his early twenties was strenuously pushing his way through the crowd toward the Ark. He was bareheaded. According to Orthodox Jewish custom, men cover their heads at all times, all the more so in a synagogue, and certainly when one approaches the apex of the house of worship where the Holy Ark is. The custom is very deeply rooted and strictly adhered to in current Orthodox practice. Its transgression in the manner of this young pilgrim would normally be considered tantamount to sacrilege. As the young man was threading his way through the crowd, people were commenting to him on his breach of traditional devotional behavior to which he replied almost pleadingly, "Yes, yes, true. But what can I do? I *don't* have a skullcap with me!" And he continued to press forward. His demeanor, sincere and pious, did not betray any lack of devotional or religious intent. To this young pilgrim it was apparently more important that he participate in the most significant act of the *hillula*—lighting the memorial light—than that he observe the commonly accepted norm of covering one's head in synagogue. As a matter of fact, the young man was not hindered or stopped by the other people present. The spirit of good humor, joy, and brotherly love that reigns at *hillulot* fosters an atmosphere of tolerance that, in this case, took in its stride the negligence of the young man. In this context people forgive behavior that would rouse their anger on other occasions.

Later at night, in the courtyard of the synagogue, two men engaged in a noisy and unpleasant quarrel. Witnesses reacted to the incident with disbelief and shock. "At the *hillula* of Rebee Hai? It is not good!" Not knowing how to deal with the situation, they tried to move away as quickly as possible, to flee the scene of what in that context amounted to sacrilege. Theoretically, people could have reacted in one of several other ways: they might have ignored what was in itself a fairly routine incident even in a synagogue, joked about it, intervened, or taken sides. Their actual reaction of shock and abhorrence was peculiar to the *hillula* situation. It contrasted sharply, yet was consistent, with the reactions to the bareheaded young man. One abhors and flees from strife, while a transgression of traditional propriety is tolerated in good humor: one does not react by causing more strife.

Generally it seems that the men in their thirties and forties were in their devotion more active and more expressive than the others. On the other hand, among the older men, in their fifties and over, at the far western end of the men's section of the synagogue, opposite the Ark, seated around the table and enjoying lustily the food and drink, there were congregants who were the mainstays of the local congregation. They were expressing their devotion by partaking of the *se'udat mitzvah* (the ceremonial meal), a central feature in many Jewish celebrations, not only at memorial rites.[7] While religious texts were being read during the meal, there was a striking contrast in demeanor between these elders seated at the table and the younger men who stood near the Ark. Many of the latter were devoutly reciting the texts; the older men were laughing, joking, and drinking. Some of them behaved frivolously, pushing dirty forks and salt into the pockets of their companions.

Though the behavior of the elders was light and gay, it does not mean that they did not take the celebration seriously. The two kinds of participation manifest, I suggest, different kinds of religious activities reflecting different kinds of social and cultural needs.

The following incident exemplifies the general piety and sincerity of one of these elders. I had greeted Rebee Frajee, with whom I had been acquainted for some years, upon his leaving the table after he had drunk a measurable amount. He said to me, "I only drink in honor of the *hillula* for Rebee Hai. Have you heard of Rebee Hai?" Then he started to speak of the saint's greatness, miracles, and piety, but his power of articulation failed him, and his words drifted off with a wistful sigh. "Ah ya ya ya, we lived with him, what a

[7] For a more elaborate description of a ceremonial meal, see Deshen 1970:140–147.

great one . . . (*anahnu khayinu ito, eize gadol* . . .)." Rabbi
Hai Taieb had lived in the eighteenth century.

The most formal aspect of the commemoration focused on
the Torah-reading table, which is on a podium in the center
of the hall of prayer. On the podium stood the distinguished
guests who addressed the crowd through a microphone.
They drew the attention of all those present, including the
reciters of devotional texts and the feasters seated at the
table. The master of ceremonies opened by remarking how
pleased he was that "we are all together here once a year, all
the Tunisians, all shades (*kol ha'gevanim*),[8] from all places,
without any difference, to honour the memory of Rebee Hai
Taieb." Then he said that those who would be called up to
light the *kandil*, the special multibranch candelabrum that
Tunisian Jews light on *hillulot*, should be generous toward
the synagogue fund. He expressed the belief that the merit of
munificence on this occasion of Rebee Hai's *hillula* would
cause the army to be victorious, and would enable Israel to
hold on to the territories that had been gained in the 1967
war. The audience participated lustily: whenever the name
"Rebee Hai Taieb" was mentioned, the cry rose from all
throats, "*Lo met!!!*" ("He is not dead!"). Mrs. Ghez, a Labor
M.P. of Tunisian origin, was the first speaker. She expressed
her joy that "we are all together here" and then proceeded
emphatically and with emotion: "And we must bless all our
soldiers that they may return in peace, and that all our
wounded recover, that all may marry and have many children, that the Jews of Russia and from the Arab countries
may soon come; that all come soon and that many children
be born here, and that we receive them all nicely (*sheniklot*

[8] In Israeli usage this idiom refers to nuances of cultural and political
differences, not to shades of color.

otam yafe), and that the state of Israel succeed and be a light for the gentiles." After each blessing the crowd roared "Amen." The speaker was continuously interrupted with enthusiastic applause, and many cried out of emotion for at the time virtually no Jews were permitted to leave Russia, and the dream of renewed contact with that persecuted community was a matter of fervent hope for all Israelis.

The master of ceremonies then invited the seven dignitaries, one after the other, to kindle the lights of the *kandil* that stood next to the reading table. Each man, upon being called up, approached the *kandil* and declared formally: "I hereby kindle a light in memory of Rebee Hai Taieb Lo Met, may his soul be elevated (*le'iluy nishmato*)." He would add particular blessings for those living that were dear to him, such as, "for the health of my wife," "for the health of my children," or "that I should make a good living." One dignitary, who was from the town of Ashdod, added, "For the blessing of all Tunisians, and particularly the Tunisian community of Ashdod."

Implications of the Data

In general structural-functional terms, the *hillulot* rituals relate to problems of the social organization and cohesion of the communities that enact them. They buttress ties and strengthen cohesion. The two *hillulot*, celebrated in the same locality within the span of a fortnight, were organized by two subgroups of the local Tunisian immigrant population, the northerners and the southerners. Between the two groups there had existed in Tunisia cultural differences, and feelings of separateness and rivalry. (This can be substantiated by historical sources.) In Ramla, where the two populations live in close proximity, the *hillulot* may possibly function as means to bind internally and to integrate the separate communities. Through the lavish *hillulot*, possible channels of competition for the two Tunisian communites in Ramla, the two communities are able to bolster their separate social structures. At the same time, however, the competition binds the competitors as Tunisians in the town of Ramla. Ultimately, the *hillulot* perhaps also function to unite all Tunisian immigrants in Israel. The Tunisians dispersed throughout the country come together on the occasion of *hillulot* from near and far to meet old friends and relatives from whom they live at a distance because of the circumstances of immigration and settlement in Israel. As one young man muttered to his neighbors when the speeches at one of the *hillulot* began to tax his patience: "Enough, enough. We came to meet people, not to hear speeches!"

This leads me to the central question. What has made these celebrations so popular in recent years? Why do people who have discarded much of the traditional way of life of Tunisian Jewry adhere to precisely this facet of tradition? The question must take into consideration the differential patterns of participation of age categories that I described above. Another important datum is the fact that many elderly, respectable, deeply pious Tunisians do not go on pilgrimage at all because they feel that on these occasions people are prone to transgressions of traditional custom and ritual, such as the consumption of food of whose ritual nature (*kashrut*) one cannot be absolutely certain, and in the mingling of sexes where there are such multitudes. The ancient religious ambivalent attitude toward memorial celebrations has not abated, and considerations such as those above arouse thought and discussion among the devout. It seems to me that with time the proportion of younger people who participate at *hillulot* is increasing. At the most recent celebrations that I attended, in December 1971, elderly Tunisians in traditional garb were conspicuously absent. The rationale for this was stated very clearly in 1968 in a sermon by a Tunisian rabbi in Israel:

We now decry in wrath and pain the new practice of holding *hillulot* celebrations in great multitudes of men, women, and children at the graveside of the pious. Whoever goes there can see with his own eyes the great festering sore of gluttonous eating and drinking, and the terrible mingling of men dressed in Sabbath finery and made-up and adorned women who attract (whether with intention or not) the eyes and hearts of the males. And what can a man then do, but sin? And is the pious man pleased at such *hillulot* . . . ? Surely he turns over in his grave in sorrow and pain! And those who arrange these *hillulot* do ill instead of good. The pious do not need their deeds, and the best thing they could do would be to restrain people from coming and to abolish these vulgar customs.   [Huri 1971:129]

I suggest that the phenomenon of the increasing popularity of the Israeli pilgrimages described here might be understood as concentrated acts of piety, in the context of the migration of people from traditional communities in Tunisia to the modern and heterogeneous Israeli social scene. During the process of migration the tenacious adherence to the many minutiae of traditional beliefs and practices is manifestly decreasing. I have the impression, based on my field of experience, that people feel that they are losing hold of the means that lead to self-justification, salvation and integrity. Participating in *hillulot* can be one way of relieving oneself of that sensation. Such participation is concentrated, dramatic, and emotion-laden, and, in the present-day social situation of the immigrants, it is far easier to take upon oneself than the discipline of constant adherence to a myriad of traditional rituals and practices.[9]

I suggest that the pilgrimages described are acts of devotion particularly suited to the needs and problems of people who have lost much of their traditional culture and social bonds. In other words they are acts of devotion of individuated people, mostly middle-aged and younger, who feel malaise in their existence. They sense to their grief that their lives deviate religiously from what they were in the past. Participation in the pilgrimages is rooted, I suggest, in a feeling of unworthiness that stems from the attenuation of traditional practice and in the problem of existence that this sensation arouses (on this point see particularly Chapter 6 below). It might provide an answer to the question—how does one attain self-justification, and thereby the sense of order and security that religion can provide? Participating in a pilgrimage possibly enhances a person's religious status in his own eyes and gives him religious self-respect. This view of pilgrimage accounts for the differential participation of various age categories. The very conservative tend not to go at all. In their eyes they probably have retained their former religious status and condemn those who go. Their religiocultural and social situation is such that they are not sensitive to the problems of existence to which the *hillula* is related. Absent also, I suppose, are people, mainly youngsters, who seek to repudiate their Tunisian ethnic and religious traditions. The majority of Tunisian immigrants probably fall between these two extreme categories. They increasingly participate

[9] For a notion of what this implies the reader is referred to any of the standard codifications of traditional Jewish practice, such as Ganzfried 1961. Participation in *hillulot* possibly comes to replace much of the minutiae of these practices.

because some of their particular problems of existence, emotional and otherwise, resolve themselves in *hillula*.

At the beginning of this study I referred to Bellah's theory of religious change. Subsequent research, particularly that of Geertz (1964), and also Colson (1971:250–252) and Singer (1972), has provided some substantiation to that theory. If my view of the *hillulot* in the light of this work is to the point, then we should now have an insight into what prompts people, like the young man who bareheaded pushed his way through to the Holy Ark pleading not to be hindered, and the other men, all in their prime, to gather in earnest devotion in the most sacred part of the synagogue. These are individuated persons who conceive their problems as particular and personal. The traditional customs and rites, rooted in the congregational and communal concept, exemplified by the elders gathered around the memorial feast table, fail to arouse them. The generation of Tunisian immigrants that is most involved in the life of the new society evinces religious change, in line with the theory that under conditions of increasing social differentiation religion evolves toward an evermore abstract and rationalized direction. The generation that is less involved, whose members, I suppose, are mostly retired and whose social life revolves around the synagogue, has not changed in the same direction. They express opposition to participation in the new *hillulot*, or else participate in a more traditional, congregational way.

Hillulot are very enjoyable affairs and to many probably also aesthetically satisfying experiences. They are celebrated with music, dances, and speeches, and one meets relatives and friends. On these occasions one also sees, and sometimes exchanges kisses and a few words with, important people, such as the mayor, members of parliament, and various prominent Tunisian figures. From the point of view of the synagogue leaders who organize *hillulot*, the numerous pilgrims contribute handsomely to the financing of their institutions. It is obvious that one need not be motivated only by religiocultural problems in order to participate in and organize *hillulot* and I do not suggest that the religiocultural explanation is conclusive. One nonreligious theme that appears very prominently in the data is the immigrants' concern with relating their ethnic identity to their identity as Israeli nationals. In the present context the discussion is restricted to the religiocultural factor and I indicate, tentatively, how it is associated with the current renascence of *hillulot*.

Pilgrims in Meron

An old Moroccan Jew

Traditional garments at a pilgrimage in Jerusalem

Singing and dancing at a Jerusalem pilgrimage

Youth celebrating at a pilgrimage in Jerusalem

Celebrating the acquisition of a new set of Zohar books

A ceremonial feast

CHAPTER 4

The Emergence of
Supernatural Explanations
for Male Barrenness
among Moroccan Immigrants

MOSHE SHOKEID

Among Moroccan Jews from the Atlas Mountains, where the idea of male superiority prevailed, only the woman was accused of barrenness in a childless marriage.[1] When these Jews immigrated to Israel, traditional patterns of family organization and behavior, such as the extended family and the woman's nonparticipation in outdoor economic activity, underwent changes that affected the status of the woman, and her position became less subordinate. Also, in their new environment, these immigrants were exposed to Western science, including medical diagnosis and treatment, which they accepted in most cases without reservations. This chapter examines the prevalent views about traditional beliefs of barrenness in a community of Moroccan Jews (the same community that I have called Romema in the earlier chapters) after the inhabitants had lived for ten years in Israel.

[1] This did not apply to cases in which the male was impotent. As long as a man seemed virile he was thought able to procreate.

Background

In Morocco, girls and married women were segregated from male company (except from the company of the immediate family); they would not join the men, even to partake of meals with male relatives. Their activities were confined to domestic pursuits and some industries, such as weaving. Except for the very old, women were constantly under the guardianship of a male relative—father, brother, or husband.

The household unit was customarily the extended family, where accommodation, occupation, and income were shared by the parents and their married sons. Upon the death of the father the extended family pattern would often continue under the leadership of the eldest brother; it split up only when the sons of the brothers married. The aged men of the family, whether father, uncle, or older brother, enjoyed an honored position. It would seem that the household unit was not properly complete without an elder figure.

Elsewhere (1971b), I have analyzed the many changes in relationships in the traditional Moroccan family which were due to immigration to Israel. There is no doubt that the rapid breakdown of the traditional extended family pattern was brought about by the new environment. In part it was compelled by the physical, economic, and social planning of the *moshav*, which was orientated toward the establishment of equal, independent, small family units. The attempt made by brothers to form partnerships and to preserve the traditional framework did not last for long, and the partnership often dissolved with much bitterness and animosity. Brothers, who in Morocco had been organized in one large unit in business and domestic life according to a family criterion of seniority of age, became independent, equal members of the *moshav*. Quarrels broke out when the equal investment in work and facilities could not be clearly calculated and the partners could not agree on a fair distribution of payment received for crops.

There is a close connection between the dissolution of the extended family and the far-reaching changes in the traditional status of women and in the traditional patterns of marital relationships. The economic cooperation of men within the framework of the extended family in Morocco made possible the relegation of women to domestic realms. With the establishment of independent nuclear families of farmers, however, women became the main source of help in outside economic activities. The majority of Romema women work regularly, together with the men, either on their own farms or on other farms for wages. This contrasts sharply with the highly specified division of labor and sexual segregation which prevailed in Morocco. The procreation of children, which had always been stimulated among Moroccan Jews by the adherence to patrilinial beliefs [2] and to Jewish mourning ritual and commemoration customs,[3] shifted into a new focus in Romema. My observations led me to the conclusion that the traditional motives for procreation in Romema were all the more compelling with the loss of the legitimate right to demand the support of the extended family (which may have included prolific brothers) in daily activities and during old age. Children were more essential to a married couple among the Romemites than they had been in Morocco, since the in-

[2] "Sterility is less of a curse in a matrilineal society than in a patrilineal society" (Turner 1968:197).

[3] Orthodox Jews greatly welcome the birth of a male child, since only a male can recite the *Kaddish*, a mourning and commemoration prayer for the dead (see Zborowski and Herzog 1964:309).

dividuated nuclear family in Romema had mainly to rely on its own resources and children either for its economic enterprise or for support during old age. I should emphasize, however, that in Romema, old parents were not abandoned to state welfare agencies, as they were in other immigrant communities, including Moroccan communities and especially those in urban settings.

During their ten years' residence in Israel, Romemites became acquainted with, and came to appreciate, Western medical services. In most cases of illness and pain, the Romemites tried to get medical help as soon as possible. The village clinic was always crowded during the doctor's twice-weekly visits. At other times they went to clinics in nearby villages or to the hospital in the regional town Beersheba. They often jokingly referred to treatment of ailments according to folk practices, speaking of these practices with an air of superiority as evidence of the improvement in their style and standard of living in Israel. Whenever Western medicine did not help the Romemites or did not assure them of permanent relief, they turned to folk healers or famous rabbis reputed to be able to intercede with heaven, and made pilgrimages to holy shrines and sites. In these moments of crisis the Romemites often tried Western and folk remedies simultaneously. Thus, for example, in a case of severe asthma, the patient who depended on continuous medical treatment also availed himself of every opportunity to consult anyone conversant with folk medicine. While medical treatment in these cases provided only temporary relief, folk diagnosis and treatment frequently (through mystical means or other ways) explained the cause of the ailment, illness, or other affliction and held out hope for permanent relief or an end to the misfortune.

The medical treatment of barrenness was more complicated when it implicated the man. There was a close relation between sterility and the deep-rooted theory and attitudes of the Romemites about the differential status and innate qualities of men and women. As confirmed by other researchers (Jacobs 1956:255) [4] and indirectly through my survey of folk tales, barrenness was attributed only to women in Morocco (Noy 1964:34). [5] In searching for evidence about the customs and beliefs regarding barrenness among non-Jews in Morocco, I found a similar attitude. While the use of sorcery could afflict Berber men only with temporary impotence (Westermarck 1926, I:571–573), it could afflict women with permanent barrenness (Westermarck 1926, I:575).

In Israel a Moroccan immigrant treated for impotency was confronted with a profound dilemma. On the one hand, enjoying the benefits of science and technology, particularly in modern farming, he also appreciated Western medical treatment in general. On the other hand, when that medical treatment concerned itself with his ability to procreate, it seriously affected his image and personal integrity as a man, threatening his status in the family and the community. In this chapter I am mainly concerned with observing and ana-

[4] Mrs. Phyllis Palgi, anthropologist with the Israeli Ministry of Health who has had much experience with Moroccan immigrants, has confirmed in a personal communication the observation that barrenness was attributed only to women in Morocco.

[5] I have searched for Moroccan folk tales whose theme was barrenness. One story (Noy 1964:34) is about a barren woman who in seeking remedy risked her life. She entered the tomb of a famous rabbi (also worshiped by Moslems who did not let Jews near the site) to implore him for children. The story opens with the following description: "A sick man and a barren woman who asked at the tomb for mercy, one found relief, the other conceived." In another tale, whose provenance is Tangiers, it is also implied that the woman was responsible for the childlessness of her marriage (Haviv 1966:35).

lyzing the course of action taken by the husband who found himself in this dilemma.
‸The research is based on two case studies. In the first and main case, the principal figures are Barukh, his wife, Ruth, and his younger brother, Yoel. Problems of barrenness, conjugal relations, and relationships between the eldest brother and younger brother combine to illuminate the complications and suffering that the change wrought in family relationships and values. The second case (presented in summary), in which the main figures are Nathan and his wife, Rivkah, deals mainly with barrenness.

Case I

Life History of Barukh and Ruth

Barukh's father died young, leaving Barukh, the eldest, then in his early teens, in charge of his mother, younger brother, and sister. Barukh, like his father, became a shoemaker. His sister married a poor but hard-working paternal cousin, and his brother, Yoel, worked for a well-known rabbi in another community and sent his earnings to Barukh. After many years of hard work, Barukh's economic position improved. He had saved enough money to buy some sheep, which were herded by a Moslem according to the usual arrangement between Jews and Moslems (the revenue of the offspring when sold being divided between the owner and the shepherd). The wealth of the rich and influential among the Jews in the Atlas Mountains was often based on the ownership of large flocks of sheep. This modest beginning started a new future for Barukh, who could now, at the age of thirty-two, afford to marry and start his own family. His bride, a ten-year-old girl, had not yet reached puberty, and their marriage was not consummated until she was about twelve. According to Barukh's evidence she conceived shortly afterward, but miscarried in a few months' time. She soon became pregnant again, and while this time she gave birth, the birth was premature and very difficult, and the baby, a girl, was born dead. The mother died a few weeks later. Barukh at times blamed himself that the child was born dead, for it happened soon after he unintentionally pushed his wife roughly away from him when she had tried to prevent his interference in a quarrel. Thus came to an end his brief marriage; Barukh often reminisced nostalgically about it. Already in his late thirties and anxious to have a family, Barukh did not accept his mother-in-law's offer to marry his late wife's younger sister who was then not yet ten years old. Instead, a year later, he married his present wife, Ruth. She was a widow, mature in years, and Barukh hoped that she would soon bear him a child. During her first marriage Ruth had had a baby, but it died in infancy; she may also have had a miscarriage. Barukh and Ruth told me that when they left Morocco for Israel in 1956, Ruth was pregnant, but she miscarried soon after their arrival in Israel. The couple believed that this time Ruth miscarried because of a quarrel they had had over some domestic matters. Ten years passed but Ruth did not conceive again, a situation about which Barukh used to say: "Since then we have been closed (*segurim*) for children." Their childlessness was a major tragedy for Barukh, and he did not fail to bring up the subject, in one form or another, at most of our encounters.

Soon after the couple's arrival in Israel, Barukh arranged a marriage for his brother, then in his early thirties. The two couples, living in the same house for a few years, continued the traditional pattern of the extended family according to which Barukh was the senior and authoritative figure. Their economic situation, however, was difficult, as it was for all newcomers. The Romemites were employed in relief work as unskilled laborers. Only heads of families were entitled to a quota of relief work, and days of work per month were allocated according to the number of dependents they had. Yoel, who was physically the stronger, usually worked both his and Barukh's quotas. Barukh soon decided to raise sheep, as he had done in Morocco. With the money he saved from his brother's and his own income, he bought a few sheep, which he herded with much care and love. During my fieldwork Barúkh and Yoel owned the best flock in the village.

After a few years, Yoel established his own household, when Deborah, Yoel's wife, refused any longer to endure Ruth's domination. In fact, Deborah left home, together with her small children, and stayed for a few months with her mother and brothers in another village. In view of her firm decision, Barukh and Yoel saw no alternative but to separate the households. On her return Yoel and Deborah moved into their own house. The separation of households, however, proved to be complicated, since the brothers had also decided to divide their economic enterprise. The brothers' maternal uncle and a rabbi, a relative who lived in a nearby village, were consulted. It was finally decided to follow Moroccan traditional custom of inheritance and to give the elder brother two-thirds of all possessions. In spite of the division of possessions, the brothers kept their livestock together. Barukh cared for the flock four days a week, and Yoel two. On the Sabbath, the herd was kept at home and taken care of by the women. When a lamb or sheep was sold, Barukh got two-thirds and Yoel one-third of the money.

When Barukh slaughtered a sheep for food, for the festivals, he gave Yoel an equal share of the meat, since Yoel at the time of my fieldwork had four children.

Since 1963 the settlement authorities [6] have allocated farms to the Romemites. In 1964, Barukh took over a farm and in spite of his apparent physical weakness was quite successful. He usually cultivated only those crops which are farmed extensively and require relatively little work, for example, sugar beets, potatoes, melons and peppers; and refrained from planting tomatoes, cucumbers, onions, and so forth, which demand much care and at times many field laborers. Yoel did not take up farming, apparently because of his wife's precarious state of health; she developed severe asthma. Instead, lacking his brother's enterprising spirit and managerial skills, he became a night sentry in a nearby village and was employed on the farm of one of the settlers in the same village. He was, therefore, unable to help Barukh with his farming. Barukh, who since the separation of households could no longer command his brother's labor, felt that he had been let down by Yoel, since the latter seemed to prefer to work for a stranger. He was apparently willing to pay Yoel for his labor, but, in fact, the two were uneasy and embarrassed that there should be a financial arrangement of wages between them. They felt that such an arrangement was humiliating for brothers.

To Barukh's great disappointment, his wife Ruth continuously refused to work on the farm. As mentioned earlier, settlement in Romema led to a drastic change in the woman's role in economic life, a phenomenon connected with the dissolution of the extended family. Although Barukh's outlook

---

[6] See the Introduction for an explanation of these administrative bodies.

was deeply rooted in traditional Moroccan Jewish culture and mores, he soon adjusted to this change in family life. His wife, however, did not conform to this change, and she disappointed Barukh's expectations to help on the farm. She claimed that she was ill and weak—a reference to her gynecological condition (a subject on which Barukh was very touchy)—and thus could not do the hard work on the farm. When he tried to force her to join him in the fields she refused categorically; she even left him a few times in protest and went to live with her brothers in another village. Humiliated and frustrated, Barukh called her back, giving in to her wishes. For his difficulties with his wife he was partly compensated by her cleanliness and her delicious cooking, which he appreciated very much.

Thus Barukh could not rely on children, or wife, or brother to help him. He had, however, a close relationship with his brother-in-law, his sister's husband. His brother-in-law was a dedicated and successful farmer who was also employed as a night sentry in the nearby village and sometimes even worked for wages on a farm there. Barukh's sister, a mother of four children, was a devoted companion to her husband and helped out on the farm. In comparison, Ruth did not seem to be a very dutiful wife. In fact, continuing and intense animosity prevailed between Barukh's wife and his sister. Both Barukh's sister and brother-in-law were so weighed down with work that they could extend little direct help to him on his farm and in other activities. Yet despite the fact that he had almost no one to depend upon for assistance, Barukh managed economically quite well.

Much of Barukh's income went into the improvement of his standard of living, despite the fact that he feared to be left destitute in his old age. He refurbished the house partly on his wife's insistence, but mainly because he liked modern appliances and the modern way of life. During my stay in Romema, he had a refrigerator, a gas cooker, a solar heater, and a washing machine, as well as a bath and an indoor toilet.[7] Barukh was also the first resident of Romema to build (during my stay) a large closed veranda which he intended to use as a hall to entertain guests. He closed off the kitchen, which had been part of the entrance hall, and turned it into a separate room. He had the most comfortable house in Romema and he convinced his brother-in-law also to rebuild and refurbish his home. Since then a few other settlers have followed suit.

Gradually, I came to realize that Barukh played an important role in the religious and leisure activities of the Romemites. Well-versed in prayers, he also knew many tunes, and he had a pleasant voice. He was often asked to lead the prayers in the synagogue. Although the Romemites were divided into three opposing patronymic groups, Barukh was frequently invited to parties of all groups, which were held on the Sabbath, the festivals, and on other festive occasions. He entertained the audience with his singing and his tales and legends about ancient heroes and scholars.

Barukh was known for his munificence. He frequently contributed substantial sums to various religious funds and charities, to the poor, and to the synagogue. His contributions, however, were largely prompted by his hope for children. His donations seemed to be a means of imploring God to give him a son. Thus he was one of the four farmers who in 1966 donated a new velvet embroidered curtain (*parokhet*) to cover the Holy Ark in the synagogue (which contains the

---

[7] The houses in Romema only had showers, while toilet facilities were in a small shed a few meters from the house.

Torah scrolls). This curtain was acquired at the time of the High Holy Days and cost IL. 1,000 (about $300). The other three contributors were among the most prosperous farmers of Romema. The contribution for the *parokhet* is symbolically related to procreation, since opening the doors of the Holy Ark is commonly believed to be conducive to opening a closed womb. (One of the other three contributors was Nathan, another man whose marriage was childless; the case is discussed below.) Quite often at the festive meals and parties Barukh went to or gave, he received the blessing that he might beget a son. The biblical story of Abraham was proffered as evidence that he should not despair. No doubt Barukh's generosity enhanced his prestige in the community and developed a public concern for his personal affliction.

Barukh's and Ruth's Search for Children

For many years Barukh had tried all kinds of methods that would help him and Ruth have a child. Charitable acts and donations were only one continuous practice. During my fieldwork Barukh was emotionally and mentally torn between the acceptance of Moroccan traditional beliefs about barrenness and folk treatment for the begetting of children, and seeking the help of Western medicine.

Barukh firmly believed that he was being punished for some past misdeed, particularly his refusal to marry his late wife's younger sister. He used to describe their barrenness as "the stopping of children" (*atzirat ha'yeladim*), comparing it metaphorically to a drought imposed by the heavens which may come to an end at any time with the will of God. Barukh's beliefs were confirmed by the rabbis and Jewish and non-Jewish folk healers whom he had asked for blessings, remedies, and miracles. He explained to me, for example, that an Arab healer from Ramla, a town with a mixed Arab-Jewish population, told him that heaven had closed his wife's womb because of a sin he had committed in the past. The same healer, however, also told Barukh that his weak physical condition was a factor which affected his children, unconceived as well as miscarried and stillborn. Barukh disregarded the latter statement and only accepted the first, which harped on his supposed guilt.

Among the different types of healers, Barukh preferred those who dabbled in magic. He was greatly impressed by another Arab healer from a village near Haifa, reputed to communicate with the powers of the netherworld, who argued with the spirits and asked them to leave Barukh in peace. The healer promised him that Ruth would conceive in two months, that his firstborn child would be a girl and after her he would have three boys. He gave Barukh and Ruth amulets to wear around their loins. Ruth, however, did not conceive. Barukh also visited a Yemenite healer but was not impressed by him. He took me along on this occasion. The Yemenite healer recommended practical measures, but first tried to find out whether Barukh and Ruth had ever reached orgasm together; apparently they had not. The healer suggested that this was due to a worm which disturbed their sexual contact and also affected their fertility. He advised that Ruth put some cotton in her vagina after intercourse, and then they should have intercourse again. He further recommended that Ruth put a spleen of a cock, wrapped in a sheep skin, in her vagina, leave it there for four days and refrain from intercourse during that time. The healer refused Barukh's request to give them an amulet and they left for home very disappointed.

Barukh's rejection of the suggestions of the Yemenite

healer who offered this practical intervention reminded me of his attitude toward the diagnosis and treatments suggested to him by doctors. Some time before my arrival in Romema, Barukh had been excited by the news that there was a specialist at the Beersheba hospital who was known for his successful treatment of barren couples. Barukh and Ruth went to the doctor through their local medical services and were very enthusiastic about the prospects. According to Barukh's story he was not diagnosed as sterile, but, he went on, the doctor suggested that he try mixing his own semen with someone else's and that Ruth be artificially inseminated with it. I assume that Barukh rejected the doctor's advice, since to follow it would have reflected on his manhood and pointed to his inadequacy. But in moments of despair, he spoke of artificial insemination as a last resort if everything else failed. I think he would have been more favorably disposed to the idea if his wife had been a more obedient companion. Unfortunately, she seemed arrogant, and at times Barukh had to remind her quite harshly who was master. Artificial insemination might have affected his image of superiority and undermined his authority at home. He once told me, in the presence of Ruth, that a man's first wife is selected for him in heaven, while his second marriage is matched for him according to his deeds performed in the world. Ruth interpreted this statement as disparagement of her. Embarrassed, she feebly denied its validity.

I finally decided to move out of my detached position and intervene, suggesting that Barukh go to a top specialist in Tel Aviv. He was very enthusiastic and asked me to make an appointment. The effort turned out to be futile, but it clearly showed Barukh's attitude toward the problem of barrenness. While he anxiously awaited the appointment, he was disappointed with the results. The couple was examined thoroughly and told to come back in a month. In the meantime, they were told to keep a record of Ruth's temperature, and to bring all documents related to their previous medical examinations. No more information was divulged to them, nor were they given any hope. Barukh did not keep the appointment and never bothered to return to the specialist.

Modern medicine, which Barukh generally valued in the treatment of ailments and disease, offered him little comfort in this most crucial matter, since medical tests either would imply that he was sterile or would call for a long and tedious treatment without any certain promise that Ruth would conceive. Barukh clearly preferred to believe that their barren marriage was a punishment from God, or misfortune inflicted by malevolent spirits whose evil might be warded off by the will of God, or by mystical means. Therefore, although he told me that occasionally he despaired, he never gave up the search—or considered the cost of it in time and money—for any person known for his religious or mystical qualities who might help him.

Barukh, however, did not reject Western medicine altogether. Rather he approached it in the same way as folk medicine. In his meeting for the first time with a noted specialist, he hoped for a short successful treatment, assuming that the doctor's reputation was based on his own particular, personal medical system. Barukh apparently did not conceive of modern medicine as an integrated system of knowledge and experiment with doctors drawing on one body of knowledge and science. Therefore, in spite of his disappointing encounters with doctors, I assume that if he had had the opportunity, he would have tried other famous doctors.

His last pilgrimage during my fieldwork was to Jerusalem

to a famous Ashkenazi rabbi, who, however, was not at home. During that visit Barukh bought a new set of phylacteries (*tefillin*) and white shrouds (*takhrikhim*) in which Jews are buried. Deep down it would seem that Barukh had given up hope of having a child, yet he could not reconcile himself to the finality of this, which meant that his life had been a barren waste. Moroccan Jewish tradition did not provide Barukh (or Ruth) with the solution allowed, for example, to a Tallensi sterile man (Fortes 1967:23–24) whose wife could beget a child by another man, or with the solution of adoption prevalent, for example, in China, India, ancient Greece, and Rome (see Goody 1969). Since Moroccan tradition accused only the woman of sterility it left Barukh only the alternative of divorcing his wife and remarrying a fertile woman. A Moroccan rabbi (who had advised Barukh and his brother on the division of their shared property), who was also a relative, reproached him for preferring good cooking (implying Ruth) to children. This accusation was leveled when Ruth refused Barukh's demand to help him on the farm and in protest went to stay with her brothers. At that time Ruth even argued that Barukh was to blame for their childlessness and that she would not return home unless he bequeathed her half of his possessions. This was thought to be a most impertinent claim (for more details see Shokeid 1971b:188–191). Barukh, however, did not divorce Ruth, and the same rabbi (who realized that Barukh was reluctant to divorce) persuaded Ruth to return home.

Barukh's reluctance to divorce was reinforced by the theory of punishment for his past misdeeds which he came to believe in and through which he recognized his own share of the responsibility for his barren marriage. Also, in Morocco he would have had a good chance of marrying a young woman, or even a girl, but no young woman would have readily married him in Israel and marriage to a mature woman made adjustment all the more difficult. He was already used to Ruth and he appreciated her housekeeping.

Semi-Adoption, Barrenness, and Family Setting

Though childless, Barukh was surrounded by children. At the time of my research, his brother, Yoel, had three boys and a baby girl. Barukh was especially attached to his eldest nephew, Eli, a clever and good-looking eight-year-old. He spent most of his time at his uncle's house, which was roomy and comfortable compared to the crowded and humble home of his parents. Eli's friends looked up to him because he spent so much at his well-to-do uncle's home. He used to say that if his parents left Romema—a possibility because of his mother's illness—he would stay with his uncle. Barukh told me, on more than one occasion that Eli was born in his own house, when Barukh and Yoel were living together. He described how he walked to the hospital with Eli in his arms when the child was seriously ill. He thus apparently saved Eli's life. It seemed to me that Barukh considered the love of his nephew preferable to artificial insemination, which might have impregnated his wife with a stranger's child who later would look down upon Barukh. Eli was a close agnate, who loved him as a son, and who was named after his father. While still trying to find a remedy so that Ruth might conceive, Barukh told me that he used to test Ruth's affection for Eli. For example, just before they were ready to sit down to dinner, he would send Eli home, speaking to him in a rough manner. He was delighted when Ruth called Eli back and fed him in the kitchen. But on one occasion, when Barukh was discussing their affection for Eli, Ruth said that once they had their own child, they would not be so open and loving toward Eli. Yoel had little control over Eli and the child barely obeyed him. Yoel, however, did not complain overtly that Eli more readily obeyed his uncle and preferred the latter's home. His wife, Deborah, once told me that Yoel was filled with a "sense of shame" (*busha*) because Barukh had no children. By "a sense of shame" she probably meant that he felt embarrassment, sadness, and even guilt. By not having a firm hand with Eli, Yoel made a sort of sacrifice for Barukh, who was much more fortunate than himself except for his childlessness. It was probably a painful irony that Yoel, apparently the less talented of the two brothers, and his invalid wife had four intelligent and good-looking children.

Barukh somewhat slighted his brother and patronized him. At times he seemed to harbor resentment toward him and showed disrespect, in that he continually refused Yoel's invitation to festive meals. Yoel was very distressed by the situation and often spoke with hurt and bewilderment, saying that he did not know what had happened to Barukh, who used to be such a nice, warmhearted, and congenial person. He observed, rightly, that whenever Barukh was persuaded to partake of the Sabbath meal at Yoel's home, he was not as convivial as he was with other Romemites. He refused to sing, talked very little, and did not praise the food. The estrangement which developed in their relationship was expressive, in part, of the present ambiguity concerning the norms of behavior between elder and younger brothers. Yoel's large family, which bestowed on him an important existential, religious, and prestigious advantage vis-à-vis his elder brother, made the situation even more difficult for Barukh. With other Romemites, Barukh, though childless, had sufficient prestige to hold his own and could accept their hospitality graciously. Moreover, on these occasions he enhanced his prestige by entertaining his hosts both as singer and storyteller. In accepting the hospitality of his younger brother, however, especially in the presence of other guests, Barukh's childlessness and his inadequacy as a male were sharply accentuated. Thus, while Barukh was "forced" to accept the hospitality of his younger brother, simply because he was his brother, he was not the same gracious guest he was with others.

In the light of what is known about the patterns of family life of the Romemites in Morocco, we can assume that if not for the changes which have occurred in the various spheres of life, due to immigration, Barukh would have been able to cope much better with the misfortune of his childless marriage. First, in Morocco there would have been no reason for the serious suspicion that it was he who might be sterile, and much of his mental anxiety and misery would have been prevented. He probably would have divorced Ruth and remarried a third time. Second, his wife would have been more obedient and respectful. She would not have dared to accuse him of sterility and would have been completely subordinate to him. Third, his brother and his family would have continued to live with him as an extended family of which he would have been the head, in the position of the older and better-educated brother. Barukh's authority over the whole extended family, both in the economic and in familial spheres, would not have been questioned, particularly with the bashful Yoel. Thus, the extended family pattern would have lessened a great deal of Barukh's anxiety. Even if he had remained childless all his life, he would have continued to be the head of a large and economically secure family. To bring a case in point, in Morocco, where the extended family was the basic pattern of family life and tradi-

tional thought never attributed sterility to man, Sarah Mahluf, the sister of Barukh's brother-in-law, was compelled to
marry her widowed and childless paternal uncle. Her uncle
had stayed with his late brother's two sons and daughter. His
nephews, fearing that he might marry a girl with whom they
would not get along and that their household pattern would
thus break up, urged the marriage. The marriage between
the aging uncle and his young niece was fertile. The old man
died in Israel a few years later, leaving behind a young
widow and two handsome boys.

Barukh was killed in a road accident, on the eve of the Day
of Atonement, in 1967. To the surprise of many Romemites,
Ruth insisted that Yoel, her late husband's brother, marry
her in levirate marriage (*yibbum*), as commanded in the Bible
(Deut. 25:5–10). The biblical law of *yibbum*, which is intended to procreate a child to carry on the memory and name
of a married man who died childless was (and is) often a
severe burden on the widow, since it forces her to marry her
late husband's brother who may be, among other things, either already married, or old, or too young.[8] Most widows
prefer to be relieved of this duty and be allowed to marry
whomever they want; this is only possible through the con-
sent and release (*halizah*)[9] of their brother-in-law. The law of
yibbum, however, is nowadays rarely enforced, if at all.[10]

[8] If the brother has not yet reached the age of legal religious maturity,
which is thirteen years and one day, he can neither fulfill the obligation of
yibbum nor give *halizah*.

[9] *Halizah* is a religious rite—the details of which are not relevant to our
discussion—in which the childless widow is released of the duty to marry
her late husband's brother. Among Orthodox Jewry throughout the world
the rite is obligatory before the woman is allowed to marry a man other
than her husband's brother. In Israel *halizah* is legally enforced in all cases
where it applies.

[10] Since biblical times, rabbis have contended about the biblical law of
levirate marriage. Some early authorities preferred levirate marriage to

At the time of these events, I was not in Israel; I assume, however, that Ruth insisted that Yoel, whom she had not particularly respected during Barukh's lifetime, fulfill the obligation of *yibbum* for reasons other than her love of and loyalty to Barukh, one of which may have been the fact that she had little chance of making a good new match since she had two childless marriages behind her. Yoel, on the other hand, even if Israeli law permitted levirate marriage, would have been reluctant to marry Ruth, since he already had to support four children and a sick wife, to whom he was greatly attached. Deborah, his wife, would not have easily agreed to Yoel taking a second wife. In short, a second wife would have caused an enormous economic burden and great emotional difficulties. Ruth could not find strong support for her case among the rabbis whom she approached. However, though she probably realized that there was hardly any chance of forcing the prolific Yoel to fulfill his traditional duty toward his late brother, her unusual demand, theoretically legitimate according to biblical law, was a dramatic plea to prove her claim that she was not to blame for her childless marriage and that she was physically without defect. Eventually, she took *halizah* from Yoel and left the village to marry another man whom she divorced soon afterward. (I

---

halizah (release), while others advocated *halizah*. In the late Middle Ages, Ashkenazi (those who follow the Franco-German Jewish rite—see Chapter 2, note 6) rabbis preferred *halizah*, since the deceased's brother might already be married and polygamy had been prohibited among Ashkenazi Jews since the eleventh century. Sephardi Jewish communities (those who adhere to that branch of ritual tradition codified in Spain during the Middle Ages), such as those of Morocco, applied both the laws of levirate marriage and *halizah*, depending on the case at hand. In Israel, however, only *halizah* is possible if the deceased's brother is already married, for otherwise he would be liable for bigamy.

have no information about either this marriage or the divorce.) A few years later, Yoel paid tribute to his late brother's memory by naming his newly born son Barukh.

Case II
Nathan and Rivkah

There were two other couples without children in Romema. One, an elderly couple, were quite alone in the village since neither husband nor wife had close relatives in Romema. The couple were considered odd. The husband was usually described as nervous and peculiar. He was often the butt of jokes among the Romemites. He did not farm, but was a day laborer on other farms. During my fieldwork the childlessness of that couple was, as far as I know, not seriously discussed by the Romemites.

The other couple were young, Nathan (29) and Rivkah (25), and apparently modern in behavior and outlook. At the time of research they had been married five years. They had married of their own choice. They worked harmoniously together on their farm, which was very successful. They often used to go out together for entertainment in nearby towns. Considering himself a modern man, Nathan aspired toward a higher standard of living. The couple had modern furniture and many modern appliances. Nathan was the first Romemite to have a flower garden solely for its beauty and for recreational purposes. However, even though the couple got along well and their economic situation was good, the general opinion in Romema was that unless they had children, their marriage would eventually break up. Nathan, who was proud of his manly appearance, often used to tease people in an aggressive manner, tell risqué tales, and indulge in obscenities. While he never discussed the question of children, some of his actions, as well as Rivkah's remarks, made it obvious that all was not well with their marriage. As a matter of fact, Rivkah regularly visited a doctor in a town near Tel Aviv. I was told by settlers from another village where Rivkah had a girl friend that, because they were childless, Nathan made life difficult for Rivkah. She was apparently ready to discuss the question of divorce, but not before Nathan himself underwent a medical examination. The rumor in the neighboring village had it that nothing was found to be wrong with Rivkah but that Nathan apparently refused to be examined. From another reliable source I was told that Nathan refused the local doctor's advice to take hormone injections. Instead, he preferred to believe that he had been bewitched by the mother of a girl to whom he had been engaged before he married Rivkah. When the girl's mother realized that he intended to break off the engagement, she practiced sorcery while offering him a drink.[11] Nathan apparently believed that only through the will of that woman, or through an opportunity to drink again from the same cup she had served him, or even from a piece of that cup if it was broken, would he break the spell which rendered him childless. A young settler, a close friend of Nathan's, who thought that the marriage of Nathan and Rivkah would not long endure if they remained childless, also told me that there was a rumor about Nathan's inability to beget children. He thought that Nathan should have a medical check up and follow the doctor's instructions. But, he went on, "Nathan is not the man to accept these things." The same settler told me that at one time he himself had considered marrying Rivkah,

[11] That report of sorcery is reminiscent of a method prevalent among non-Jews in Morocco to make a woman barren (Westermarck 1926, I:525, 526).

but he was very glad that he had not done so. (He married another girl who had already given him three children.) The last statement confirms the general attitude still prevailing in Romema, which considers women either capable or incapable of bearing children regardless of their husband's fitness. The statement was made by a man who himself said that Nathan might be at fault in the question of having children. Some people said that Nathan forced his wife against her will to work on their farm, and on other farms for wages. Apparently someone had overheard him say to Rivkah that since she had no children what else could he do with her.

Nathan's attitude toward religious life was ambivalent. For example, sometimes he showed his indifference to religious ritual by leaving before the end of the service. On the other hand, some of the biggest donations to the synagogue and to visiting poor scholars were contributed by him, partly in the hope that he might be rewarded with children. He was one of the four farmers, including Barukh, who, in 1966, donated the new velvet embroidered curtain to cover the Holy Ark of the synagogue. Once a year a session of reading the Zohar was held in his home. Nathan and Rivkah also went quite often to the holy tombs of Meron and Safed to which people wanting to be helped and healed were drawn from far and wide. Nathan gave out as a reason for these frequent visits that they were going to see Rivkah's brother who lived in a village near Meron. This pretence exemplifies Nathan's uneasiness in his search for a means to beget children, since he followed a custom usually practiced by barren women (see Noy 1967:34).

It is probably significant that at the evening prayers which heralded Rosh Ha'Shanah (the Jewish New Year) in 1966, Barukh led the prayers, while Nathan contributed a large sum to the fund of the synagogue for the privilege of being the first to open the doors of the Holy Ark. Thus, the two men who were childless were performing the main public roles during the service of this major religious festival, when it is said that the fate of every Jew is being weighed and decided upon by God.

Although Nathan was much younger than Barukh and had served in the Israeli army, where he had been exposed to Western thinking, and although he married of his own choice, his behavior was not much different from that of Barukh. At that stage, he appeared to be even more reluctant than Barukh to consider any nontraditional practice and treatment which might have cast a doubt on his virility. (Although I have not engaged in a study of the difference between the two men, the fact that Barukh was much older and therefore possibly felt that time was against him might be considered here.) Nathan, however, was ambivalent in his relation to his wife. She was a full partner in his various undertakings. He respected her opinion and gave her responsibilities. They probably were also the only couple who used to go out regularly together for entertainment outside the village. But in Romema, Nathan never took Rivkah along to festivities and she never joined the table when he was entertaining guests at home, at a time when an increasing number of women in Romema sat at the table in the presence of guests, and some even occasionally joined their husbands when invited to the homes of other Romemites for a meal.

In spite of the prediction made by a few Romemites during the period of my fieldwork that the marriage of Nathan and Rivkah would not last if they did not have children, they were still married when I visited Romema five years later (in

1972). At that time, Nathan was still refusing medical treatment. Talking with another young couple about the medical treatment of barrenness during my 1972 visit, the woman pointed out with disdain that there was something unnatural about the use of hormones. She thus seemed both to explain and to justify Nathan's refusal of medical treatment.

Supernatural Explanations: A Step toward the Acknowledgment of Male Sterility

In this chapter I have examined the course of action taken by childless husbands who were brought up on the "male ethos" of the male's mental, social, and biological superiority, and who suddenly, under the impact of the scientific world, were confronted with the dilemma of consulting a physician regarding the cause of their childlessness. Their hesitancy to undergo medical treatment has been analyzed as the outcome of the fear that medical diagnosis may show and make publicly known that it is they, the men, who physically are responsible for their childlessness. This blemish on their virility may undermine the image of the man whose undoubted fertility is one of the mainstays of his superior status in the family and community.

The main finding, however, is that both Barukh and Nathan were ready to acknowledge that they might possibly share in the responsibility that they had no children because of some kind of mystical punishment inflicted either by God, or, preferably, by dark powers from the netherworld, or by persons who practiced sorcery. But the implications of accusations of sorcery, which were brought up in these cases, are different from those observed on some other occasions in Romema that resembled the phenomena of witchcraft and sorcery as reported particularly among many African societies.[12] On these other occasions and in African societies, it was observed that beliefs and practice of witchcraft and sorcery called for an active reaction by both the victim and the accused to remove the malevolent consequence. In contrast we find, first, that both men mentioned moral sins they had committed as the cause of their punishment and misfortune. Thus, Barukh refused the offer of his late wife's mother to marry her younger daughter. Nathan, on the other hand, in breaking his engagement to the girl, brought down on himself the wrath of her mother, since he had shamed both the girl and her mother. Second, both mothers were now dead and could not relieve their victims of the sorcery they had practiced, nor could they pardon them. It appears as if both Barukh and Nathan were ready to accept moral responsibility for their misfortune.

Although the men were the primary cause of the childlessness, however, the continued barrenness was only partially their fault, because the agents of mystical retribution had died, thereby becoming invincible forces. The fact that the situation could not be resolved, since it was beyond the powers of the healers, who commanded usual means of mystical and divine intervention, added an element of tragedy to their affliction. Therefore it was fate, rather than their manhood, which had failed them.

In fact, Barukh and Nathan spoke openly about the circumstances of their moral responsibility for their childlessness, although it had not yet been made clear that it was they alone, and not their wives, who physically were unable to beget children. The acceptance of their moral responsibility

[12] See for example Gluckman's introduction to Kuper's play (1970) which deals with the problem of barrenness.

can be seen both as a mechanism of self-protection by the patient against the shock of a possible medical diagnosis which would show his physical deficiency,[13] and as a protective mechanism against public opinion, which was generally affected by modern life and no longer accepted traditional attitudes unquestioningly. In both cases, however, there were no supernatural explanations proffered for the physical condition of the woman. She was considered either capable or incapable of bearing children regardless of her husband's fitness. It is important to note that Moroccan rabbis and healers, whose help had often been solicited for other misfortunes related to health and family relationships, were not called upon by the Romema men to help in the begetting of children or to provide an explanation for childlessness in marriage. The only role played by Moroccan rabbis was that of urging Barukh to divorce Ruth. Thus the official attitude, as represented by Moroccan traditional leadership, still identified the woman as the only party responsible for barrenness. Therefore the acknowledgment of moral responsibility and the search for supernatural explanations for barrenness by the rank and file of Moroccans, as represented by Barukh and Nathan, who were also reluctant to divorce their wives, seems to me a compromise with traditional attitudes. Under the new economic, social, and cultural circumstances, these men faced new and acute problems of ultimate meaning. It was through innovation in the supernatural—a realm which before had not been relevant to the question of barrenness— that they were able to create an existential position whereby they could face the anguish of a new dilemma, rooted in a rapidly changing world, and thereby symbolically resolve

[13] See Palgi's report on the mental breakdown of a Yemenite Jew upon hearing that he was sterile (1966:80–81).

that dilemma. The particular predicament of these Romema men also revealed the broader challenge—gathering momentum in their society—to primordial images and systems of symbols and beliefs. The Romemites' response to the issue of barrenness thus constituted a step forward toward the acceptance of the reality of Western medical diagnosis, the acceptance of a situation where there is greater equality in the actual status of women, and the acknowledgment that the innate qualities of men and women are relatively equal.

CHAPTER **5**

The Situational Analysis of Symbolic Action and Change

SHLOMO DESHEN

In the course of investigating the change in religious beliefs and practices of immigrants from rural Tunisia and Morocco in Israel, I initially sought to conceptualize the phenomena encountered in terms of "secularization." This chapter is a consequence of the problems that arose.

In the first section I discuss some of the general problems inherent in the sociological use of the term "secularization" and of the closely related church-sect typology. An approach to the study of religious change which attempts to solve the problems that have been raised is suggested in the second section. The third section presents a case study to illustrate this approach.

Sociological Use of the Term "Secularization"

Sociological literature often considers religious change in the light of the church-sect typology and of the term "secularization." Troeltsch (1931, first published in 1912) initially conceived church and sect as two distinct and opposing types of religion, in the doctrinal as well as in the organizational sense. The universe of religions that Troeltsch sought to illuminate through these concepts was that of contemporary and of past religious groups of Christian Europe. Subsequent works on the subject by such scholars as Niebuhr (1929) and Pope (1942) helped to focus attention on much new data drawn from the American religious scene. Thus if Troeltsch's categories were to remain useful in the conceptualization of empirical data, they had to be redefined. The tendency of many sect-type religious groups to change and to attain characteristics of church-type religious groups was one of the most important findings that emerged from the American studies, such as those of Niebuhr and Pope. Incorporation of these findings into Troeltsch's typology meant a reformulation of his terms. The opposing categories of church and of sect came to be conceived as opposite poles on a continuum of religious groups, implying a polar conception of "religion" and "secularism" and introducing a dynamic component. This dynamic component has in more recent research (particularly that of Pfautz 1955) been termed "secularization." Pfautz, in seeking to explicate certain sociological dimensions of secularization, such as changes in the demography, ecology, and the social structure of religious groups, conceived of "secularization" as a dynamic social force at the root of the movement along the sect-church continuum which mediates between the poles of "religion" and of "secularism."

   This general line of sociological thinking—that is, the continuous redefinition of terms in the light of new data—no longer meets the needs of empirical research. The various reformulations of Troeltsch's concepts that have been suggested (e.g., Johnson 1957, 1963, Berger 1958) are, because of the wealth of new data, so radical that their empirical use distorts cultural reality. Thus Johnson (1963), for instance, is logically driven to categorize Catholicism and Orthodox Judaism in America as more sectlike than the major Protestant denominations of America. Such a conclusion runs counter to all conventional, historical, and literary uses of the terms "church" and "sect." Troeltsch's original terms, which were purely descriptive, have become infused with radical new content. While there is no logical flaw in this line of thinking, it needlessly complicates the language of sociologists. It may be simpler and semantically clearer to create neologisms with which to convey the new content and to set aside the original terms belonging to an earlier stage in the development of the sociology of religion. More fundamentally, formulating problems arising from new sociological interests in terms and with the tools of a past stage of sociology can hinder analytical imagination and drive new thought into given grooves.

The church-sect typology and the concept of secularization inherent in it conceive of religious change as rigidly polar, with "religion" and "secularism" at opposing ends. In recent years, this conception has been challenged by many quarters. Yinger (1963) states the need to differentiate between religious changes of various kinds, and stresses that "secularization" is not congruent with religious change generally. Scholars, such as Martin (1965), Matthes (1962), and particularly Shiner (1967), severely criticize the use of the term "secularization" in sociology and point to its ambiguous uses in current empirical research. In the light of recent research, the problem concerning the terms "sect," "church," and "secularization" has become fundamental. Basically they are ethnocentric and descriptive terms, initially developed by scholars rooted in liberal Protestant theology, and they were first applied to European Christian data. Particular cultural and religious conceptions cling to the terms, causing the attention of the research to focus on particular phenomena and particular evaluations of phenomena. Hence the difficulties that sociologists of religion have encountered when applying the church-sect typology to studies of non-European Christian religions. Similar difficulties emerge with any attempt at a cross-cultural use of the term "secularization." Wilson (1966), examining the Anglican Church decisions on the problem of birth control, conceptualizes the increasingly liberal attitude as an instance of "secularization." A comparative examination of such decisions in a different socioreligious context, such as that of Judaism, might also show an increasingly liberal attitude. Phenomenologically, however, the two cases need not be two similar instances of "secularization." Accounts per se of a change in practice are often meaningless; the general socioreligious context must also be considered. In the present example, one would need information on the legitimization of the change. Change in religious practices can be rooted in casuistic mechanisms inherent in canon law to enable change; the same changes can sometimes be devoid of such traditional control and legitimization. Information on the motivation for change is also relevant, specifically with reference to the degree and manner in which tradition is disregarded.

As a result of work done in the past fifty years, and of the confusion pervading the empirical use of the term, "secularization" is often given a general sociological meaning. Pfautz's use of the concept "secularization" as an analytical frame according to which differential social properties of religious groups can be discerned attributes to the concept the general sociological content of "social differentiation." There are, however, phenomena peculiar to culture and religion as a particular sphere of action within society, which, as I argue in the following section, are best conceptualized by concepts evolved from action in the sphere of culture and religion. Therefore, to discuss properties of religious groups in analytical terms that are used in general sociology must necessarily have a baneful effect. It detracts from the study of particular religiocultural phenomena and focuses on problems of formal institutional analysis only.

There is a final objection to the current sociological use of the term "secularization." The polar conception of "religion" versus "secularism" implies that "processes of secularization" are dominant and widespread among religious phenomena in modern societies. Such an assumption, together with vagueness as to what precisely is meant by "secularization," is an abortive factor in research in the sociology of religion. The assumption leads away from questions that should be central: namely, what is religion in modern society? What are the varieties? What are the changes? The question whether religion in modern society is or is not "secularized" should be left open and the problem should be posed in different terms.

An Approach to the Study of Religious Change

A general approach to a solution of the problems raised should, it seems to me, consist in the forging of conceptual tools of a more abstract analytical nature. These tools must illuminate the central question of the study of religious change: "How does religion change?" The concepts, which must be derived from the study of religion itself, should permit for the differentiation of particular phenomena within the sphere of religiocultural action. They will thus, first and foremost, illuminate the religiocultural sphere itself. The field of inquiry must be narrowed down to elemental components of religiocultural action.

This brings us to the need for a working definition of religion. Drawing on Geertz (1966), I offer the following definition: A religion is (1) a system of symbols (2) that refers to problems of ultimate meaning and (3) thereby formulates an existential order.

(1) "A symbol" I see as the expression of a sentiment or sentiments through concrete form (such as, articles of belief and ritual acts).

(2) "Problems of ultimate meaning" are problems that confront man and remain with him when he has reached the limits of understanding. They are problems that arise in times of great stress or at times of moral reckoning and they include questions of suffering and moral consistency. They are found in situations where chaos threatens to intrude and shatter an ordered conception of existence.

(3) By "formulation of an existential order" I have in mind a systematic configuration of symbols that is an effective mechanism through which the individual orders his experiences.

The definition is very broad and can encompass phenomena of symbolic action in many fields other than religion, as traditionally conceived, such as science, art, and ideology. This is possible, provided that the symbolic actions are related to the formulation of an existential order vis-à-vis problems of "ultimate meaning." If one accepts a definition of religion along such lines, it follows that a sociological understanding of religion entails primarily the examination of symbols and systems of symbols in relation to the varied and changing situations of the people who carry the symbols. Coming to the problem of religious change, one would want to know how and why particular worshipers change the meaning that they attribute to religious symbols, and how particular religious changes are related to particular life situations and social roles. For purposes of empirical research our analytical categories will be constructed by focusing on the actions of religious worshipers in relation to particular symbols.

In recent years, there have been many outstanding studies of religious change that focus on the analysis of changing symbolic actions. Very few of them, however, have tried to differentiate between the various phenomena of religious change. Among those who have is M. Marriott (1955:esp. 191ff.), who, following the work of Srinivas (1952), uses the concepts of "parochialization" and "universalization." Willis (1968) establishes the categories of "amalgamation" and "splitting" of "behavioral elements." In another paper (Wyllie 1968), a typology of symbolic changes comprising "change," "jettison," and "introduction" is suggested (see also Waal Malefijt 1968:355).

Despite their usefulness, these formulations represent only rudimentary attempts to order the mass of data on symbolic change. The formulations which evolved out of descriptive ethnocentric data are subject to the criticism made earlier in this chapter. They also lack a firm basis in a theory of symbolism; the typologies are arbitrary, and in their formulation the particular nature of religious phenomena was not taken into account.

The fourfold typology of symbolic actions below is an attempt to take research in the field today further, to arrive at greater clarity, and to refine the tools used. The typology, which is rooted in the definitions of religion and symbols stated above, seeks through a greater degree of abstraction to encompass phenomena cross-culturally. It comprises the following categories: (1) eradication, (2) creation, (3) innovation, and (4) profanation. "Eradication" and "creation" are actions that pertain to the formal expression of the symbol. They are diametrically opposed: "eradication" is an action whereby a symbol is eliminated; by an act of "creation" a new symbol is wrought. In acts of innovation and profanation the formal expression of the symbol undergoes no change; the acts, however, impinge on the meaning and content of existing symbols.

Eradication

An act of eradication consists in the separation of a symbol from the range of existential experience to which the symbol traditionally applies. This occurs when the worshiper ceases to carry out the action that a living relationship with the symbol implies: the symbol thus loses relevance to experience. When the worshiper refrains from a ritual action, he eradicates the ritual so far as his personal religiosity is concerned; also, when the worshiper ceases to believe in a particular article of faith, he eradicates the set of symbols that composes that article of faith. Stated concretely, it means, for example, that when a tribal African ceases to relate his anxieties to the power traditionally attributed to witchcraft, he eradicates witchcraft.[1]

Eradication, as a category of religious change, is a very common phenomenon in modern society, but it needs special

---

[1] These formulations imply criticism of the category of "ritualism" (or "formalism") that is often used in theological literature. "Ritualism" usually means the adherence to traditional forms that lack content. The term is often used derogatively, implying legalism, pettiness, lack of religious thought and feeling. However, the execution of symbolic actions that are irrelevant to existential experience is logically inexplicable. "Ritualism," therefore, cannot stand as a category of religious action. What appears superficially as "ritualism" will in fact, I assert, emerge, upon close examination, as traditional symbolic actions that have undergone changes, and that I categorize presently as either "profanation" or "innovation."

emphasis. Many of the functionalist theoreticians seem to be reluctant to face the empirical datum of eradication. Davis (1948:543), among others, argues that "there is ultimately a limit . . . how far secularization can go . . . otherwise the population . . . is not likely to stick together sufficiently to maintain order and protection." This functionalist dogma has been challenged by many scholars, such as Spiro (1966). The focus on religious symbols shows that ultimate eradication is empirically possible. This is well documented in Firth and Spillius' (1963) restudy of "The Work of the Gods in Tikopia." Although "the work" as a whole has not died out, many particular rituals and parts of rituals have fallen into disuse, and the cycle of rituals as a whole has become constricted.

Creation

An act of creation consists in relating a range of existential experience(s) to a symbol which is either newly created or adopted from an alien tradition. Great historical figures of traditional religions sometimes created symbols. Acts of creation can also be found in such phenomena as religious conversions, "political religions" (described in general by Apter 1963), and in modern gnostic cults. Below I cite an illustration from Geertz's description of a Javanese funeral and of the subsequent rites (Geertz 1957). The death here is ritualized by a group of people whose local leaders adhere to politicocultural ideas in which nationalism, Marxist politics, and a stand for indigenous Javanese syncretism against Islam are combined. Geertz describes the local leader's commemorative speech as follows:

He went on . . . building up a whole rationale for the present national political structure on the basis of a mystical interpretation of

President Sukarno's 'Five Points' (Monotheism, Social Justice, Humanitarianism, Democracy and Nationalism) which are the official ideological foundation of the new republic. . . . He worked out a micro-macrocosm correspondence theory in which the individual is seen to be but a small replica of the state, and the state but an enlarged image of the individual. If the state is to be ordered then the individual must also be ordered; each implies the other. As the President's Five Points are the basis of the State, so the five senses are at the basis of an individual. The processes of harmonizing both are the same, and it is this we must be sure we know. [p. 46].

In effect what the orator does is to relate the experience of a person's death to a particular ideology, in which, as Geertz's account shows, the experience of death is ritualized. In the performance of funerary rites the religious parlance of Islam was traditionally used. In the present instance, however, the orator disregards it and instead explains and formulates the experience of death in novel symbolic terms. This is an act of religious creation.

The derogatory categorizing by many writers, both social scientists and theologians, of such phenomena of religious creation as "pseudoreligions" and "secular religions," seems to me unfounded. There is no logical reason to consider the symbolic actions and beliefs of these modern religions to be in any way different from those of traditional religions, provided, of course, that the experience of the symbols is genuine (in the sense of the definitions given at the beginning of this chapter). To attribute a diffuse symbolic value, which relates to problems of ultimate meaning, to scientific or artistic activities, is theoretically also an act of religious creation. But lack of empirical research in this field renders it terra incognita for the present.

Innovation

An act of innovation consists in changing the range of experience to which a symbol applies. The symbol becomes infused with new content that pertains to a range of experience previously not expressed by the symbol. The general category to which the newly symbolized range of experience belongs has previously been expressed by the symbol; now, however, the symbol has widened its connotative scope, since it also comprehends the new range of experience.

Illustrations of "innovation" are legion. I cite one example from Judaism. Traditionally, the study of the Mishnah, the ancient Jewish code of canonic law, was conceived as an act of piety expressive of a desire to commune with the realm of the divine. In late medieval Jewish mysticism, however, the act of studying Mishnah became imbued with additional content. It was deemed to benefit the souls of the dead, and it therefore became a central part of the ritual of memorialism. The desire for communion with the realm of the divine evolved into the particular desire of communion with the souls thought to inhabit that realm. The general category of ranges of experience relevant to both the traditional and the mystical study of Mishnah is the same. The differences are in the change of details within that general category. Such acts of religious change I categorize as acts of innovation.[2]

Profanation

Like innovation, profanation is an act which consists in changing the range of experience to which a symbol applies.

[2] For further illustrations see Scholem 1965; also Ames 1963; Geertz 1964; Peel 1968; and the studies mentioned on p. 157.

The symbol also becomes infused with new content that pertains to a range of experience previously not expressed by it; in the case of profanation, however, the general category to which the newly symbolized range of experience belongs has not been previously expressed by the symbol. Here lies the difference between profanation and innovation. As there is little empirical documentation on the phenomenon, I shall illustrate it more elaborately. The following is an illustration from my own observations. According to one of the rules of Jewish ritual law, one may not "decrease the sanctity" of ritual objects. In concrete terms this means that, for instance, a receptacle in which phylacteries have been placed may not be used for a prayer shawl, which, for reasons that do not concern us now, is an object of the lowest degree of sanctity (*tashmishey mitzvah*), lower than that of phylacteries. And, of course, one should not place in a phylacteries receptacle objects of daily secular use. On the other hand, the container of a prayer shawl may hold phylacteries (Karo 1960:37). Discarded ritual objects must be disposed of in ritually prescribed ways, which differ according to the degree of sanctity.

In recent years Israeli manufacturers of prayer shawls market their wares in cheap polyethylene bags, as is customary in the clothing and linen trade generally. The buyer usually discards these bags—permissible in this case, since the ritual sanctity of prayer shawls is of the lowest degree. On the polyethylene bags of the *Talitania* prayer shawl factory are imprinted traditional symbols that often are embroidered on velvet prayer shawl bags. Beneath the symbols appears the message: "This bag should be used only for *Talitania* products." In the atmosphere of religious change current in Israel, there are definite signs of increasing orthodoxy and ramification of ritual in certain traditional circles, which the *Talitania* factory uses to its advantage. In such an atmosphere the suggestion that prayer-shawl bags be considered akin to ritual objects to be disposed of carefully and respectfully is accepted innocently, though according to binding *halakhic* law this is nonsense. What the *Talitania* manufacturer is doing, perhaps even consciously, is to extend the *halakhic* admonition concerning the use of ritual objects to a commercial situation where it does not strictly apply. The manufacturer thus conveys an ambiguous message. He expresses the traditional ritual admonition in very concrete terms suited to the context; thereby he also draws attention to the products of *Talitania* as such. The ritual message serves as an advertising means to the manufacturer. It has been infused with content from a range of experience that is foreign to the relevant rittual admonition in its authentic form.

An article by D. E. Peven (1968) on American home-party sales organizations also provides delightful illustrations of the same phenomena:

A home-party is the gathering of women in the home of a "hostess" for the manifest purpose of being entertained but for the actual purpose of being sold merchandise by a saleswoman. . . . The living room is converted into a sales room . . . the guests play games and are served refreshment; and the dealer . . . tries to persuade the guests to allow the future use of their homes for a similar purpose. . . . The tone of the meeting is similar to that developed by evangelistic religions, and the emotions of the audience are deliberately evoked and manipulated by techniques such as mass singing to create a collective consciousness and identification with the companies. [pp. 97–98]

In the course of these activities, traditional symbols were infused with content that pertains to commercial activities. The dealers were specifically told by their managers "to arrange the chairs in the living room so that the guests face the products as if on an altar" (p. 99). Traditional concepts also undergo similar change: "The sales counselors and the president pointed out again and again during the meeting of dealers, that the only thing necessary for success was to 'believe in' the product, to 'believe in' what it can do. . . . 'If you do what we tell you to do and come to all of the meetings you will be rewarded. . . . You are lucky to be one of us because when you are one of us you are "saved." Now go forth and carry the "word" ' " (pp. 103–105).

The texts are saturated with American Protestant revivalist symbols, both idioms and technique, such as "belief," "salvation," "word," and the general sermonlike approach of the managers. These are used to convey commercial messages not even remotely akin to the theological messages they traditionally evoke. The changes that these symbols underwent at home-party organizations and the change of the Jewish regulations concerning ritual objects I categorize as "profanation." I use this value-oriented term deliberately, because the actions that are covered by the term are illegitimate when viewed from the aspect of the traditional religion in a given context. The question as to the degree of the traditional legitimization of any particular action of religious change is of analytical importance. When I state that the general category of experience now conveyed by the symbol had previously not been expressed, I do not refer merely to a quantitatively far-reaching stage of religious innovation; rather I seek to isolate a type of religious change that is so out of range, that the traditional religion has, in a given particular context, no traditional mechanism to legitimatize it.[3]

A Case Study—A Torah Scroll Presentation

The pivotal concepts in my presentation have been "symbol" and "existential experience," and I have argued that action relating to symbols must take into account the relevant existential experience of the actors. Phrased in more operational terms, symbolic actions and the social situations of the actors compose a single unit; religious change must be examined in the light of that one unit, forming a single field of inquiry. The necessary technique is to handle ethnographic data through "situational analysis." [4]

The case that I propose to study along these lines consists of a ritual that was performed during the 1965 general election campaign in Ayara. The incident took place at the height of election campaigning, when political parties vied with each other to dispense favors to potential voters.[5] It occurred during a Torah scroll presentation to a synagogue congregation of recent immigrants from Morocco that I call Shevah Yisrael by *Pai,* one of the parties that ran in the elec-

[3] See also the case study in the following section and Elkin 1969. A good historical example is the atheistic medieval interpretation of the classical gods; this interpretation enabled pagan gods to survive through the era of Christianity (Seznec 1953:11–36; Cooke 1927).

[4] Situational analysis consists of examining series of related data in order to deduce from them patterns of regular action. Empirically, the data are examined as units, such as "extended cases" and "social situations"'(see for instance Van Velsen 1967, Mitchell 1956, Turner 1957; for a concise methodological statement concerning situational analysis in the field of symbolism see Gluckman 1965:260–261, and for its application see Turner 1967).

[5] For details see Deshen 1970, chs. 2, 3, and 6 in particular.

tions. Torah scrolls are the most valued artifacts of the Jewish religion. Each synagogue is required to have at least one. There is a shortage of Torah scrolls in Israel because hundreds of new synagogues have been built since the onset of mass immigration in 1948. One of the main ways of attaining scrolls is through custodians of the property of Jewish communities in the Diaspora that have become defunct, either as a result of massacre by the Germans during World War II, or as a result of assimilation. A political party frequently helps to provide a synagogue with a scroll through its contacts with these custodians; the party seeks thereby to influence the vote of the congregants.

An Israeli Ritual

On the evening appointed for the Torah scroll presentation, the whole Shevah Yisrael congregation and many other Moroccan immigrants belonging to other congregations were assembled outside the *Pai* branch, at the far end of the town. The children and many grownups held lighted torches which were made from tin cans secured to sticks with nails and filled with kerosene-soaked rags. The Torah scroll was carried in the center of the throng. The men constantly pushed toward the scroll in order to have the privilege of carrying it a few yards; this privilege was granted to practically all the adult males. Throughout the hour-long procession, the festive Sabbath Eve hymns as well as other hymns were chanted. Women along the way respectfully stopped when the procession passed them. They piously raised their hands to their eyes and kissed them repeatedly. The flicker of the torches in the dark and the excited chatter of the children who milled around on the periphery of the crowd radiated a peculiarly religious atmosphere of solemn rejoicing and restrained emotion. The crowd finally arrived at the synagogue and, to the sound of exited and devotional chanting, the scroll was placed in the Ark. Everybody then sat down to listen to speeches: *Pai* helps people to maintain their beliefs; here in Ayara a scroll is brought to the synagogue for the enhancement of tradition; the same is done in other towns and villages; everywhere *Pai* helps people to remain religious vis-à-vis rampant secularism and the efforts of secular parties.

The last speaker brought the tone to a climax, closing his harangue with the dramatic impassioned call: "Hear O Israel, the Lord is our God, the Lord is One (*ehad*)! This is the D, the great D, the D of *Pai!* Vote D! (*Ze ha'daled, ha'daled ha'gadol, ha'daled shel Pai! Hatzbiu daled!*)." The assembled crowd then proceeded to the regular evening service, which included the invocation just quoted, a verse that forms a pivotal part of the Jewish prayer services.

The symbolic action on which the analysis is focused is the worshipers' expressive declaration during the service of the ancient Jewish monotheistic call, "Hear O Israel, the Lord is our God, the Lord is One." Two distinct sets of actors are engaged in the symbolic action of the declaration of faith of the evening prayers: the *Pai* politicians and the congregants of the synagogue. They are, however, involved in contrasting social situations. I suggest that these social situations differentially mold the meaning and the character of the symbolic action in which both sets of actors are united.

The verse "Hear O Israel . . ." forms the central credo of the Jewish faith. It appears originally in the Bible (Deut. 6:4), whence it came into the daily prayers, and is repeated at least three times a day. This is one of a very small number of prayers which Jewish canon law obligates the observant Jew to recite with devotion and concentration (*kavana*). Most prayers, even if recited perfunctorily, are deemed acceptable, but the credo of the Jewish faith must under no circumstances be said without due devotion. Throughout Jewish history, the most intense religious fervor and passions have been focused on this ancient monotheistic call. These emotions erupted particularly at times of crisis and ultimate sacrifice. Generations of Jewish martyrs, from ancient times down to World War II, died with this verse on their lips. The obscure archaic phrase lends itself readily to manifold interpretations. The verse is the recognition of the one God, but it is also a supplication to Heaven, an assertion of identity with Jewry, a cry of defiance aimed at tormentors, an affirmation of moral life in the face of ruthless death—and it may be all of these simultaneously. Indeed, a literature of rabbinic homiletics has accumulated around this single verse. There is a traditional form in which the credo is written, and preserved, in the script of Torah scrolls: the final letters of the first and last words of the verse are written in larger characters than the rest. All prayer books have adopted this form, and these letters are also printed in a type bolder than the rest. The election symbol of *Pai*—the Hebrew character for "d"—happens to be the same letter that is made prominent in the credo.

The politician thus trod on highly emotional ground when he made his appeal for the assembly to vote for the "d" of the credo. The speech was timed so as to climax a religiopolitical ceremony—the procession and the Torah scroll presentation—in a way, to be the opening to the regular evening service that included the recitation of the credo. All the worshipers, both the congregation and the politicians, were observant Jews and ritually they were bound to focus their attention on this recitation. It may be presumed [6] that the particular political interpretation that had just been suggested was upermost in the minds of the worshipers and impressed itself further in the course of the ritual recitation. Thus an analysis of the ritual must take into account the election speech that preceded it.

Let us now examine the symbolic action of the recitation of the credo at the evening service from the point of view of the politicians. The notion they wanted to convey with the political speech was essentially this: The ancient credo, like the Torah as a whole, is pregnant with hidden meanings, which are constantly revealed to new generations that seek to immerse themselves in the Holy Writ. *Pai*, whose election symbol "d" coincides with the "d" of *ehad*, is the party that represents all that is right and good in the eyes of the Lord, by virtue of this coincidence.

In effect the speaker manipulated the credo for purposes of electioneering by interpreting in a homiletic manner the boldly printed "d" character of *ehad* so that it was seen to be related to the election symbol of the party that happened to be the letter "d." The election speech was delivered after religious emotions had been stirred by the procession, the hymns, and the presentation of the Torah scroll, and it preceded a religious service in which the credo must be recited with due concentration. The aim of *Pai*, a religious party,

[6] The phrase indicates a deficiency in the quality of the field data at this point; here I rely either on logical deductions or on informal impressions. Obviously, this is undesirable, for if I am wrong, my interpretation will not stand. My present aim, however, is not to analyze this particular ritual for its own sake, but rather to demonstrate the feasibility of this general approach to ethnographic data in the field of religion. It certainly necessitates uniform high quality field data.

aside from the aspirations of its members for political power, is to succeed in elections in order to execute religious policies. Thus it is reasonable to assume that the motivation of the politicians was essentially religious.[7] In this instance, the politicians fired emotions by a homiletic interpretation of the credo that suited propaganda purposes. It is a characteristic feature of traditional Jewish homiletics to use symbols, particularly biblical verses, as vehicles to convey topical socioreligious messages. The aim of these messages is to enhance loyalty to what the preachers conceive as traditional Judaism.[8] The preacher thereby changes the meaning of the symbols, albeit in a traditionally legitimate manner—legitimate because the constant uncovering of new meanings in the Holy Writ is inherent in Jewish homiletics. Rabbinic homiletics are in effect a mechanism for religious innovation in Judaism. The speech of the *Pai* politician, wherein he attributed political content to the credo, is in this context a religious innovation. This analysis also applies to the politicians' declaration of the credo during the evening service. It is a religious innovation.

So far I have focused my analysis on the change that the ritual call "Hear O Israel . . ." underwent in the prayer of the politicians. Now I turn to the worshiping congregation. I have the impression,[9] based on a general knowledge of the people involved, that the congregation did not see the aims of the religious party in the same light as the politicians. The congregants are all newcomers to Israel, mostly naïve and unlearned, to whom free party politics and democratic elec-

---

[7] This assumption is also based on a general knowledge of religiopolitical life in Israel (see Eisenstadt 1967:309–320). See also note 6.

[8] Katz 1961, ch. 17.

[9] See note 6.

tions are novel. They do not differentiate very clearly between the various motivations and aims of the different parties. All parties and all politicians are strange to them, and the highly complex phenomenon of an Israeli religious party is baffling. From the point of view of the worshipers, the salient fact that resulted from the election speech was that their experience of the symbol of the credo on the occasion of the religious service that followed the Torah scroll presentation was colored by an interpretation they could not relate to anything traditional. The whole set of activities connected with the elections was entirely new to them. They were confronted with a novel interpretation of the symbol related to a strange political context. When the congregants came to practice their devotions at the evening service, the political interpretation that had just been suggested must have been on their minds. Seen from this aspect, the ritual action that took place at the evening service is an act of profanation.

I have analyzed the ritual actions of two sets of actors. The actions take place within a single social field: public prayer in synagogue.[10] The general social situations of the various actors are, however, very different. These situations cause the significance and meaning of the actions of the various actors to be analytically different. This level of detailed analysis is possible only when clearly delimited actions, and the

[10] I have pinpointed my analysis on the ritual recitation at the evening service. As Dr. H. Goldberg has pointed out to me, a similar analysis could be made by focusing on the speech of the politician. The speech can be seen as a communal act, even though only one person cites the verse and voices its interpretation. One might argue that listening to the speech also constitutes participation in the ritual. The advantage of this perspective is that it obviates the assumption that the audience carried the interpretation in their consciousness from the time of the speech till the ritual recitation about five minutes later.

social situations in which they are enacted, are conceptually embraced and discussed as a unit.

I conclude in a polemical vein. Analysis of ritual action that does not also confront the complexities of social situations affords understanding only at an abstract and general level. In approaching the incidents discussed in this case study with the conventional terms of sociology of religion, one might characterize the incident as a whole, the speech and the prayers of both politicians and congregants, as "secularization." But in fact, as we have seen, the sociocultural contexts are such that the actions are diverse. Only by distorting the diversity can the actions be encompassed by a single analytical concept. The situational analysis of the symbolic action generates analytical tools of a finer texture than the concept of "secularization"; the case study demonstrates that a single symbolic action may convey different meanings to the persons involved in it, depending on the differential individual social situations of the actors. By focusing both on symbolic actions and on their contexts, we gain analytical concepts of a general nature that encompass many phenomena and that are incisive enough to conceptualize particular phenomena of religious change. We are relieved of the burden of ethnocentric concepts and are able to analyze phenomena in more universal terms.

CHAPTER 6

The Varieties of Abandonment of Religious Symbols

SHLOMO DESHEN

In view of the decreasing fruitfulness of sociology of religion in the Weberian tradition, many sociologists and social anthropologists have shifted their attention from Weberian concerns to questions internal to the religious sphere. Such questions center on the phenomenological nature of secularization as a religious process and entail close analysis of the changes that particular religious symbols, beliefs, and rituals undergo. The degree to which worshipers in a given society retain, or abandon, the various manifestations of the symbols of their traditional faith is one of the variables that these scholars consider pertinent to the question of secularization. Abandonment of religious beliefs is considered an index, par excellence, of secularization that, according to them, needs no further explanation. Thus Robertson in a discussion of types of secularization explicates the variables of his typology, but of "abandonment" he says merely that it is "self-explanatory" (Robertson 1970:236).

Is it true, however, that "abandonment," or as I have termed it "eradication," of a religious manifestation can be used empirically as a variable in the delimitation of secularization as a universal phenomenon? Under given religiocultural conditions, those pertaining to medieval Judaism for example, an instance of abandonment of a religious norm, such as the biblical injunction against taking interest (on money, and so forth) in commercial affairs, need not necessarily be classified as secularization. Medieval Judaism was characterized by the functioning of casuistic mechanisms inherent in traditional Jewish canon law (*halakhah*) that legitimated many changes: one of them was the abandonment of that particular biblical precept (for details see Katz 1961, ch. 8). In order to understand such religious change it is essential to consider the kind of internal legitimation, or lack of it, on which the change is based. Under religiocultural conditions where casuistic mechanisms for change do not operate, "abandonment" will be a very different kind of phenomenon; indeed, it might constitute secularization. The existence of such religiocultural differences strictly limits the use of the variable of "abandonment."

The variable was originally formulated by scholars within the religiocultural context of highly urbanized western Christian countries where casuistic mechanisms of canon law were not very potent; the acts of abandonment in such environments may perhaps be considered as an index of secularization (every situation should be seen individually to admit of the application). It would be ethnocentric, however, to approach phenomena in other religiocultural contexts by merely isolating the formal aspect of the act of abandonment and characterizing it as "secularization." For a given concept, such as "abandonment," to become useful as a sociological variable it must incorporate elements relevant to the kind of social situation to which it is applied.

Under given conditions the abandonment of ritual actions, instead of being acts of "secularization," may actually be the opposite. They may, paradoxically, be evidence of a continu-

ing attachment to the religious values related to the ritual actions. I arrived at this view in the wake of my fieldwork in a
synagogue congregation of Tunisian immigrants, Tzidkat
Hayim, in the town of Ayara.

The Tzidkat Hayim congregants originate mainly from
southern Tunisia and the core members from the island of
Djerba.[1] Southern Tunisian Jews proudly maintain their
particular identity within East Maghreb Jewry. The Jewish
folklore and special customs of southern Tunisia are particularly rich. In recent decades the religious status of southern
Tunisians has risen in their own eyes, and in the regard of
other East Maghreb Jews, because most of the religious functionaries of the area originated from Djerba and its vicinity.
This development reached its zenith when a Djerban rabbi
became chief rabbi of Tunisia.[2] Behind this phenomenon lies
the fact that until the mid-1950s Djerba was less influenced
by Western trends than other parts of the Maghreb, where
traditional Jewish education and scholarship had begun to
deteriorate.

Participation in the synagogue entails financial obligations,
and despite their very modest station in life the congregants
contribute magnanimously. Their generosity thus allows for
the enlargement of the premises and the renovation of the
synagogue. A class in religious studies consisting of twenty
to twenty-four children of the congregants, age six to twelve,
is held in the synagogue every afternoon. The teacher is paid
monthly by the congregation. The children are taught the
rudiments of Bible and ritual according to the particular tra-

---

[1] See Deshen 1969a and 1970, ch. 2, for a general introduction to the
locale.

[2] For an outline of a social history of Djerban Jewry see Deshen
1965:69–74.

dition of southern Tunisia. The congregation also engages a popular village preacher, who twice a week comes a considerable distance to discourse on homiletics and ethics at the synagogue.

The homely and pleasant atmosphere has ramifications extending beyond the confines of the synagogue. Numerous festive gatherings take place in the homes of the congregants on such occasions as commemorations of the dead and festivities related to rites of passage. The women of the congregation also interact very frequently, even though they rarely attend services. It has become a custom among many Ayara women from Djerba to gather regularly in one of the homes early Saturday morning and to gossip while the men attend Sabbath service. The old men tend to have a circle as well and after weekday evening prayers often remain squatting in the doorway of the synagogue drinking beer mixed with wine. The children who attend the synagogue classes often form play groups. All these are social activities which, although not strictly synagogue affairs, are based on and sustained by common participation in the Tzidkat Hayim congregation.

The southern Tunisians of Ayara, particularly the adult generation, generally adhere strongly to traditional practices. This is truer of them then of immigrant groups from other parts of North Africa, such as northern Tunisia and Morocco, not to mention immigrants from industrialized European countries. The fundamentals of ritual law, such as the Sabbath rest, dietary laws, and daily prayers are kept by practically all southern Tunisians of Ayara. In other ritual matters, however, much has changed and many traditional practices tend not to be performed or, at best, to be performed perfunctorily. Thus public weekday prayers have partly ceased to take place. Many people are lax in their devotions: they are frequently absent and when they do come they are often late and chatter during service. Abroad, many congregants participated in traditional adult study groups (*arba amot halakhah*) that were of central religious import; in Ayara there is very little interest in such activities. Religious practices governing marital life have also changed. Birth control is being practiced in contravention to tradition. The strict southern Tunisian customs concerning the seclusion and separation of wives from their husbands during and after menstruation are being discarded and the more lenient customs of European Jewish tradition are becoming popular. Nevertheless, observant people, though they themselves are lax in the practice of certain customs of secondary ritual importance, are disturbed when they witness the desecration of the Sabbath and other fundamental breaches of tradition in their immediate surroundings, sometimes even among the members of their own families.

I now turn to describe three instances of abandonment of ritual symbols:

The *Nefilat Apayim* Rite

According to most Jewish liturgical traditions, including that of southern Tunisia, in the morning and afternoon weekday services there are a prayer and rite called *nefilat apayim* ("the falling of faces"). The leading verse in the version current among southern Tunisians reads: "Merciful and Compassionate One, we have sinned before You; have mercy on us and save us!" Since ancient times it has been customary to recite this and other verses while leaning forward, facing the table or bench with the head buried in the arm. According to Lurianic Kabala, a major trend of Jewish mysticism that became popular in the early seventeenth century (see Scholem 1955, ch. 7), and which has greatly influenced the ritual of southern Tunisian Jews, the rite of *nefilat apayim* is invested with a profound mystical action. While performing the rite, the worshiper is believed to lower his soul into the somber depths of evil and by an act of intense concentration of thought he rectifies some of the evil of creation.[3]

The rite is very rarely practiced among the southern Tunisians in Israel. During my work with southern Tunisians throughout the country, I have observed many at prayers but have seen only two performing the rite of *nefilat apayim;* I have been told of a third man who supposedly also enacts it. I was informed that in Tunisia the number of persons who performed the rite was not large, but it was certainly not as small as in Israel. In Ayara no one does it, but the Djerbans assured me again and again that abroad many more had practiced the rite than in Israel.

Talit Katan

The *talit katan* is a rectangular ritual garment resembling a small undershirt with specially prepared woollen threads attached to the four corners. The sixteenth-century code of ritual law concerning the *talit katan,* to which the southern Tunisians consider themselves bound, reads as follows: It is good and proper that everyone should take care to wear the *talit katan* all day (Karo 1960:21). Following the code that it is "good and proper," but not obligatory, to wear the *talit katan* all day, abroad only pious and venerable men had put it on, the majority had not. Among southern Tunisians in

---

[3] For details see Scholm 1965:133, Tishby 1960:113–134, esp. pp. 128–130, and sources such as Abihassera 1967:181–185.

Israel, the wearing of the *talit katan* has become even rarer; it is in fact most unusual. A number of men told me that abroad they had regularly worn it, but had given up the custom in Israel.

Beard Shaving

Practically all the congregants, even the very old, shave regularly, at least once a week. This is in marked contrast to their slovenly and disheveled general appearance. In southern Tunisian Jewish culture, growing a beard is associated with piety and many had worn beards abroad. This is attested by verbal evidence and by photographs. In Ayara even devout congregants and highly respected religious functionaries are clean-shaven. Elsewhere in Israel several rabbis that I am acquainted with who originate from Djerba are also clean-shaven, though they are very traditional in their ideas and in their personal style of living.

Can these three instances of traditional practices falling into disuse—of religious symbols being abandoned—be taken as evidence of "secularization"? Following the position outlined in the introductory remarks to this chapter we must now consider the data within their religiocultural and social context.

The congregants are deeply aware of the decline in their religious stature since leaving Djerba. The leader of the synagogue, while describing how elaborate the preparations for festivals had been abroad in comparison with the current hasty preparations, remarked succinctly, "The merit of abroad has left us! (*Zekhut shel hutz-la'aretz halakh mei-itanu!*)." Many people, including those who discarded various customs, are deeply nostalgic about the traditional life and culture they have lost. There is a general pervasive feeling of dejection, failure, and self-depreciation in religious matters which affects the devout and the less observant alike.

The three instances of change in symbolic action just described should thus be viewed within the framework, and interpreted within the terms, of pervasive feelings of religious failure and self-depreciation. The rite of *nefilat apayim*, wearing the *talit katan*, and growing a beard are considered seemly for men of high religious status. But the manner of living and of behavior to which the people of Ayara were accustomed in the Diaspora are disappearing in the new society. Even the pious of Ayara have adopted some new ways. They and their wives have discarded the traditional dress; their young unmarried daughters no longer cover their hair as a sign of modesty; their weekday prayers are rushed; and the saintly rabbis who used to guide them are dead. The new ways, however, are adhered to only superficially. By and large they lack legitimacy both in the eyes of those who have adopted them and in the eyes of those who have not; for the recent immigrants from Tunisia have not yet developed a clear ideology or moral code to rival, let alone supersede, the consistent and affective code of traditional Judaism. Though people might ignore the example and teaching of rabbis and elders, they still revere them and their memory because they have not developed a clearly articulated alternative image of moral leadership. And therefore, while people might adopt new ways, widely divergent from those of tradition, they cannot, when confronting themselves, help but see themselves as sinners. They do not feel at one with themselves; there is a fundamental moral unease. In short, the statement "the merit of abroad has left us" is only too true. What is relevant to my present purposes is the fact that their existential situation is such as I have outlined.

This existential situation creates a problem for the congregants of Tzidkat Hayim. The *nefilat apayim* rite, wearing the *talit katan*, and growing a beard are no longer traditional activities consonant with the view that the congregants have of themselves. *Nefilat apayim* is a rite compatible only to those steeped in mysticism, or at least to "the righteous," and it should not be performed by ordinary people, since it can endanger their souls. If religiously unworthy people perform the *nefilat apayim* rite, they are apt to lose themselves in the realm of evil and cause grievous harm to their souls. The Ayara people do not now consider themselves of a sufficiently high religious stature to follow the rite. Wearing the *talit katan* and growing a beard are cases similar in point. The recurrent explanation proffered by concerned individuals was that they were "ashamed" (*mitbayeish*) to have the appearance of a pious person—undoubtedly because they felt unworthy. But it is precisely because the pious people of Ayara continue to accept the traditional meanings of these symbols that the symbols cause malaise.

A readjustment was therefore required whereby the situation would again become internally harmonious, and where there would again be a consistent rapport between the symbolic action and other aspects of the existential situation of the actor. Theoretically, this could have been done in a number of ways. The congregants might have attempted to revive all their old traditions, customs, and folkways. This the people of Tzidkat Hayim did not do. Alternatively, they might have attributed new meanings to the traditional symbols; this they also did not do. In actuality the people of Tzidkat Hayim solved the problem by effacing the dissonant symbols. They thereby harmonized their symbolic religious expression with other aspects of their existential situation. Simultaneously, however, they acknowledged to themselves, at the deepest religious level, that they had fallen from their former pious state.

It is intriguing to know more about the people who do not conform to the pattern that I have been discussing, namely, southern Tunisians who adhere to the customs I have described. The two men whom I have observed performing the *nefilat apayim* rite are both unusual and remarkable. One of them, Rabbi David, is a scion of the noblest family of *kohanim* (priests) of Djerba. Abroad he was in the center of religious, social, and cultural activities. In Israel, Rabbi David is the venerable rabbi of a village near Ayara and is recognized by southern Tunisians as their senior spiritual leader. Most remarkable about him is his uncompromising religious zeal, which he pursues to a degree quite unusual among Djerban rabbis. Let me recall one striking incident. The Organization of Immigrants from Southern Tunisia, which is headed and managed by Djerbans of noble lineage and personal piety, held a feast on a festive occasion. About fifty men participated; they included all the leading rabbis and other major figures of the southern Tunisians in Israel. Of all the rabbis and notables present, only Rabbi David refrained from partaking of the food that was served because of misgivings concerning its *kashrut* (ritual lawfulness). In effect the food was certainly *kasher*, but since Rabbi David had the slightest apprehension concerning the meal's ritual lawfulness, he refrained from eating it.[4] In other religious

---

[4] Apprehensions concerning minute points in ritual law that govern ensuing actions is a phenomenon familiar to sociologists of Judaism. For a study, largely devoted to that theme, which was carried out among a group of New York Jews see Poll 1961.

matters as well, Rabbi David is markedly outspoken and extreme. The second man is Rebee Moshe,[5] a prominent young
man of priestly lineage from the village of Binyan. The people of Binyan are involved in religiously motivated disputes
with various bureaucratic organizations; in addition, their
relations with neighboring villages are strained. Rebee Moshe
is a man of unusual strength of character and wields great
moral authority in his village. He is the moving force in the
disputes of Binyan (see Deshen 1966, 1969b).

As far as their personal religious life and actions are concerned, neither Rabbi David nor Rebee Moshe has cause to
feel dejection, failure, or unworthiness. They both react
forcefully, the one through extremism and zeal in specifically
ritual matters, the other by placing himself in the forefront in
local agitations that are religiously motivated. Both men have
reason to feel satisfied with themselves in the field of religion
(insofar as a believer in any transcendental religion can at all
be satisfied with himself). They are very active in their attempts to control their existential situation; they do not drift
with the current, but endeavor to live their lives according to
their own terms. They confront their problems with pride
and resourcefulness, hence their confidence and courage to
perform the rite of *nefilat apayim*.[6]

Conclusions can now be drawn. Can the abandonment of
the three southern Tunisian Jewish symbols be analyzed in

[5] I differentiate between the titles "rabbi" and "rebee" (see Deshen 1970,
ch. 1).

[6] There is a tendency among southern Tunisians for individual families
to nurture particular religious activities. Hence it might be argued that the
individuals discussed are just following family traditions. It is therefore
worth mentioning that the brothers of Rebee Moshe who live in Ayara
never perform the rite.

terms of "eradication" of religious manifestations? Can these instances of abandonment be seen as indicative of secularization of the religion of southern Tunisians generally? In the previous chapter I argued that a phenomenon such as the declining belief in the power of witchcraft by many Westernized Africans consists essentially in the separation of witchcraft as a system of symbols from the experience of anxieties that traditional Africans attribute to the power of witchcraft. Such a separation effectively eradicates witchcraft as a system of symbols and it is this particular phenomenon which is evidently what sociologists of religion have in mind when they associate "abandonment" with secularization. The southern Tunisian symbols that I have discussed are also related to a particular experience, namely that the actor feels himself to be righteous, worthy, and pious. In Ayara the relationship between this feeling and the symbols no longer obtains, consequently the symbols are disappearing. There is, however, a substantial difference between the African and the Ayara instances. In the African instance, witchcraft is eradicated because there have been changes in the way anxieties are controlled, perhaps even in the very sensation of various kinds of anxieties. These changes penetrate to the root of African religious beliefs, and the process is thus interrelated with profound cultural upheavals. In the Ayara instance, the experiential change is on the surface; it relates only to how the actor senses his current religious status which, being different now from his former position, is no longer in harmony with the symbol. It does not, however, reach to the bases of his religious beliefs. It is possible to argue that in the Ayara situation the abandonment of symbols which express high religious status is consistent with the continuing attachment to the religious values to which these symbols are related. The abandonment is evidence of a live relationship and interaction between the people of Ayara and their religious symbols.

The Ayara Djerbans do not abandon all their religious symbols. Why, within the orbit of synagogue services, should the *nefilat apayim* rite specifically have been abandoned? It is a sorry sociology that dismisses such questions on the assumption that we are facing simply a process of random abandonment. I am attempting to uncover the dynamics of the process of abandonment in Ayara, and in that context suggest that the abandonment of symbols relating to high religious status ought to be discussed separately from other kinds of symbols. The distinction is warranted as long as the social context in which the actors operate remains as I have described it. It is likely, however, that in time there will develop among the immigrants a new and coherent system of ideas that will legitimatize secularity and irreligion.[7] People who have abandoned the old ways will then cease to see themselves as sinners, or as religionists of low status. We would then have to analyze data such as that discussed here in different terms, possibly in terms of eradication.

I further maintain that had the Ayara Djerbans not abandoned, or more exactly not effaced, these symbolic actions, but continued to adhere to ancient symbolic manifestations of high religious stature under the new conditions, then indeed "secularization," or more precisely "profanation," might have been involved. Such continued adherence would prob-

[7] Such a situation in a different but comparable historical context has been described by Jacob Katz (1961, part 3), in his analysis of changing European Jewry during the eighteenth-century Enlightenment.

ably have entailed either a radical change in the meaning attributed by the actors to the symbols, or a radical change in
the actors' conception of the nature of religious stature itself.

I therefore suggest an elaboration of the typology, and a
distinction between two types of abandonment of religious
symbols or, phenomenologically speaking, between two
types of separation of symbols from existential experience: (1)
the separation resulting from profound cultural upheavals
and change of world views; for this I use the emphatic term
"eradication"; (2) the separation resulting from more limited
circumstances where the social change does not impinge on
basic values; in instances of this kind I suggest that the
weaker term "effacement" be used. "Effacement" and "eradication" are thus phenomena of very different sociological
conditions and circumstances.

My analysis of the phenomenon of abandonment of religious symbols by Ayara Djerbans is consistent with the
analysis of a remarkable African ritual phenomenon by Mary
Douglas (1966). I draw the relationship between the abandonment of symbols by Ayara Djerbans and the ritual abandonment of symbols in African rituals. At the core of the
most sacred rituals of various African societies there are actions that express contempt and disparagement of the article
of belief or of the object of normal devotion. In some extreme
cases the actions are destructive and bloody, such as the ritual of the Dinka and the Ndembu; in other cases, among the
Nyakusa and the Lele, they are less so. But despite the varieties of intensity of expression, the phenomenon remains analytically the same.

I cite Douglas' analysis of a Lele ritual. Lele culture focuses on the dichotomy between human and animal characteristics and qualities. Various physical, moral, and ritual

properties are attributed to these two categories of beings fundamental to the Lele world. A Lele villager is deemed to fare socially according to the degree to which he has and adheres to the putative attributes of the human category. The Lele dichotomization stimulates abhorrence of animals considered bizarre because they have traits which deviate from the norm of the cultural definition of animals or of a particular category of animals. One such freak animal in the Lele world is the pangolin (the giant scaly anteater), a hybrid monster in which all normal Lele cultural categories and conceptions are zoologically confused. The ambiguous pangolin, by its mere existence, exposes and brings into question the fundamental symbolic conception of Lele culture, the dichotomy of living beings. Yet, strikingly the central feature of one of the major Lele ceremonies is the solemn and ritual consumption of the normally avoided pangolin.

"The pangolin cult," writes Douglas, "is only one example . . . of cults which invite their initiates to turn around and confront the categories on which their whole surrounding culture has been built up . . . they confront ambiguity in an extreme and concentrated form. They dare to grasp the pangolin and put it to ritual use proclaiming that it has more power than any other rites. So the pangolin cult is capable of inspiring a profound meditation on the nature of purity and impurity and on the limitation on human contemplation of existence" (Douglas 1966:169–170).

The ritual is thus a rejection of the prevailing norm. It is essentially a confrontation with the fact that the dichotomy posited by the Lele culture is nonexistent and that the categories accepted as normal lack reality. For the brief duration of the ritual the Lele villager experiences a world that is not organized by his culture; he glimpses chaos and thus senses his own frailty. The ritual sharply focuses an awareness of the normative cultural dichotomy as it appears in ordinary Lele life, not, however, to disparage the norm, but rather to reinforce it. The effect of this rite in a traditional society, such as the Lele, that presumably does not value change and does not wish to change, is to bolster the familiar and sure concepts that have been traditionally received. In experiencing the pangolin ritual the worshiper becomes deeply conscious of his impotence vis-à-vis the dictates of his culture.

I maintain that there is a parallel between the abandonment of symbols in these African rituals and the abandonment of symbols of the Ayara Djerbans described above. In both instances, symbols are abandoned under special conditions so that they may be reaffirmed under everyday prevailing conditions. In the African instance a particular symbolic action, the avoidance of beings whose proportions and characteristics are deemed ambiguous, is temporarily abandoned in deference to the requirements of a particular religious rite which serves to reaffirm the norm through temporary abandonment. In the Ayara instances particular symbols affirming high religious status are abandoned altogether under the new local conditions. I propose that the function of this abandonment is parallel to that suggested in the analysis of the African data: that the traditional Djerban view of the actors as to the nature of piety and religious status is buttressed by the particular abandonments.

There are, of course, also very substantial differences between the Lele and the Ayara instances. The pangolin ritual is of central import to Lele religion, whereas *nefilat apayim* and the other rites mentioned are not of remotely comparable importance in Judaism. Also, the Lele ritual data are taken from repetitive or calendrical situations, whereas the Ayara data are taken from a particular point in time in a situation of social change. These differences in substance, however, only underline the analytical similarity of the data: the fact that particular symbols are felt not to conform with the experiential situations of the actors and are therefore "effaced"; while at the same time the prevailing world views and cultural conceptions are not only not questioned, but are reinforced.

The various ways in which religious symbols are abandoned can be differentiated only through a study of the changes in symbolic action within the relevant social and cultural contexts, and not through an analysis of the symbols in isolation of their contexts. This kind of study might fruitfully advance sociological studies of religious change.

CHAPTER 7

Ethnicity and Citizenship in the Ritual of A Synagogue of Tunisian Immigrants

SHLOMO DESHEN

A characteristic social development among many first-generation immigrant groups in Western countries, particularly in the United States, has been the emergence of "ethnic churches." [1] In Israel the phenomenon is also common. Of the hundreds, perhaps thousands, of synagogues established in Israel during the period of mass immigration of the 1950s and 1960s, the majority can be characterized as "ethnic synagogues." The synagogue congregations tend to crystallize around a nucleus of individuals who, originating from a particular locality abroad, maintain the specific shade of Jewish ritual tradition they have brought with them, in which they feel at home. They nurture special melodies, customs, and sentiments of communality, and they speak among themselves their native language or dialect.

The old practices, however, are not rigidly adhered to. Like other aspects of immigrant life, ritual also undergoes change. In this study I examine the nature of ritual changes that occur in the ethnic synagogue. I am particularly concerned with the relationship between these changes and the

[1] Of the many studies one might mention see Herberg 1960, Frazier 1964, Tavuchis 1963, Busia 1966.

tension between citizenship and ethnicity, which is a general problem of Israeli society.

Israeli society consists of people who, to a considerable extent, are rooted in the cultures of the countries from which they originate. People who were born in a country such as Tunisia have a great deal in common with one another, culturally and socially; the same applies to persons originating from a country such as Rumania. The bonds of common culture and origin are cohesive factors within the ethnic group. Together with existing bonds of traditional culture, there emerge new bonds of Israeli nationhood that bind all these people together; at first glance, however, the two kinds of bonds often seem conflicting. Israel does not have a clearly articulated ideology that legitimizes cultural pluralism, such as has existed for a long time in the United States. The ideology of the "melting pot" was very potent in Israel during the years of peak immigration. It is only in recent years that a more pluralistic approach seems to be becoming popular, yet ethnic loyalties and adherence to ethnic practices on the one hand, and Israeli nationalism, patriotism, and citizenship on the other, still remain uneasy bedfellows.[2] In this chapter I discuss the nature of the relationship between these various loyalties and priorities as they came to be expressed in the ritual of an ethnic synagogue.

Problems of Ethnicity

Many of the immigrants who have come to Israel in recent decades stem from relatively homogeneous, technologically underdeveloped, and generally traditional societies. Traditional religious values and practices were considered binding

[2] See, for instance, the discussions in the symposium on "The Fusion of Exiles" (Eisenstadt 1969).

as a matter of course in these societies. While there were those who strayed from the norm, the historical sources indicate that they would have been considered, and also would have seen themselves as, sinners or deviants. Therefore, theoretically at least, tradition was paramount.

Immigration to the young, dynamic, modern state of Israel was for these people a great upheaval. This cataclysmic change involved the abrupt disappearance of familiar political and judicial institutions. In the spheres of livelihood and education they were also confronted with a novel situation in Israel: only rarely did these immigrants make their living in their new home as they had done in their old one; in matters of education they had to adapt to new institutions and ideas. Least drastic were changes in family relations and in religious affairs. The immigrants established and attended synagogues of their own special traditional ritual shading wherever they settled in Israel. The veteran Israelis who ran the immigration services showed relatively little concern for domestic and religious activities. In comparison with other spheres of activities, such as education and economics, their policies in domestic and religious life were not very pronounced. No ideology demanding drastic change in these spheres existed as it did in matters of livelihood, politics and social organization, and education.

Nevertheless, for the individual who is a member of an ethnic synagogue in Israel, particularly when he has never migrated prior to coming to Israel (and this is true for a large portion of Israeli society), the experience of participating in an ethnic synagogue is new and often perplexing. The ethnic synagogue is one of the fields of social life that focuses the change in the immigrant group; it is indicative of what the immigrant retained and of the changes in his situation. In the past the social identities of members of autochthonous Jewish communities living in the midst of Gentile majorities were shaped by two basic factors: being Jewish and being a minority. As a consequence, the internal social organization of people, in the form of synagogue communities, did not normally follow ethnic lines.[3] In Israel, at present, Jewish society is much more differentiated than it was in many Diaspora communities in the recent past. Many people also do not adhere to religious practices and are not affiliated with synagogues. Those Israelis who do adhere to religious practices (and the many newly built synagogues attest to their numbers) congregate mainly in ethnic synagogues. These emerged in the course of migration to and settlement in the new country because individuals identified themselves as immigrants from a particular country or a particular locality within a country.

I proceed now to discuss certain aspects of the Tzidkat Hayim synagogue from which I draw the data for the present analysis. The Tzidkat Hayim congregants number about sixty households with a total membership of about 280 persons. The synagogue, officially called "The Tzidkat Hayim Synagogue of Immigrants from Southern Tunisia," is more heterogeneous than the name implies. Of the sixty constituent households, twenty-nine originate from southern Tunisia, nineteen from northern Tunisia, six from Morocco, four from Tripolitania, and two from Algeria. The southern Tun-

---

[3] In populous Jewish communities, social differentiation was primarily on ecological and lineage bases: synagogues existed on the basis of neighborhood and/or kinship ties. In Eastern Europe synagogues emerged which were based on a more complex pattern of differentiation—economic (synagogues whose members belonged to different economic strata and had specific occupations); religious (synagogues of various sects). For a general discussion of the historical background see Katz 1960, 1961.

isians form the social backbone of the synagogue: they were the founders and they continue to provide the leadership and the most active laymen. The twenty-nine southern Tunisians are themselves internally differentiated according to the main Jewish communities of the region. Seventeen of them originate from the island of Djerba and twelve from the town of Gabès and surrounding mainland villages. At its establishment in Ayara in the late 1950s, the active members of the Tzidkat Hayim congregation were newly arrived immigrants from the town of Gabès in southern Tunisia. The atmosphere in the synagogue is homely and the relationship among its members genial.

Symbolic Responses

I now present a series of symbolic actions pertinent to the problem of the relationship between ethnicity and citizenship that occurred in the Tzidkat Hayim congregation:

The Naming of the Synagogue

One of the worthiest ways in which Jews commemorate the dead is to establish a synagogue in their name.[4] Concrete expression is thus given to the religious sentiments of the pious who seek to honor and respect the Torah and the traditional scholars of the Holy Scriptures whose moral conduct exemplifies the Torah. The synagogue Tzidkat Hayim (literally "The Righteousness of Hayim"), founded in the late 1950s, was named in honor of Rabbi Hayim Huri, the last rabbi of the community of Gabès in Tunisia, who died in Israel in 1957. Calling the synagogue after the Rabbi of Gabès on the one hand fulfilled the symbolic function of con-

---

[4] For a brief general discussion of Jewish memorialism see Zenner 1965.

cretely expressing the religious sentiments of the congregants; on the other hand, the act was a concrete demonstration of the influence and power of the Gabèsans, who in the 1950s were the most prominent members of the congregation. When I arrived on the scene in 1965, the congregation of Tzidkat Hayim had changed. Immigrants from the island of Djerba had joined the congregation in increasing numbers and had risen in prominence vis-à-vis the Gabèsans to such an extent that no Gabèsans remained on the synagogue committee by then.

Also, Djerban Jews have notable rabbis whom they revere and respect to a degree that far surpasses their ability to articulate the sentiment. It was only natural that the Djerbans would want to express their feelings for their eminent dead in commemoration, best realized through the naming of synagogues. However, the synagogue they were attending was not called after one of their distinguished scholars. Besides this fact, Djerbans and Gabèsans are constantly competing for influence in the Tzidkat Hayim congregation: the competition is mild, tempered by mutual joking, but it is there. Thus an element of dissonance emerged in the situation of the congregants in 1965, since the social experience of the Djerbans, who by then were the prominent and influential members of the congregation, was incompatible with the absence of symbolism for their religious sentiments (in continuing to have the synagogue called after a rabbi from Gabès and not after one of their own).

The incongruity could have been resolved in a number of ways. The Djerbans might have attempted to rename the synagogue after one of their own dignitaries. As far as I know this was never suggested. Alternatively, the congregation might have split and formed separate Djerban and Gabèsan synagogues. This course of action was also not taken. Another possibility was to cease attributing active symbolic significance to the actual name of the synagogue. Again this did not happen. The name remained meaningful to the congregants. Instead the Djerbans symbolically expressed the changed social situation in the synagogue by interpreting the synagogue's name homiletically.

In 1965 the Djerban leader of Tzidkat Hayim, Perfect Sage Rebee Yosseif, explained to me that *Hayim* ("HYYM"— in Hebrew, vowels are not indicated by letters but by signs under the consonants) stands for the initials of four well-known deceased Djerban rabbis: Rabbi *H*uita (Kohen), Rabbi *Y*osseif (Berabee), Rabbi *Y*osseif (Bukhriss), and Rabbi *M*oshe (Khalfon Kohen). One of these was his own ancestor. This new interpretation coexists with the original meaning of the name that the Gabèsan members of the synagogue continue to attribute to it. The Djerban interpretation extended the connotation of the old name, adding new meaning to it, so that it became relevant to, and consistent with, their social situation as prominent synagogue members. This particular interpretation of a symbol, the name of a synagogue, is only one example of a type of homiletic manipulation that is very common in local culture.[5]

The one symbol has now become meaningful to Djerbans and Gabèsans alike. It is a vehicle through which both can express their deferential feelings toward their dead and through which they can honor the memories of their respective saintly rabbis. Significantly, the two divergent interpretations of the name of the synagogue are not voiced on formal occasions, nor do they exist in writing. There are no con-

[5] For other examples of the art of homiletic manipulation see Deshen 1970, ch. 7.

frontations between these interpretations, and the name thus remains definably ambiguous. This equivocalness can be understood in functionalist terms (though I am far from suggesting that this is the only way to approach the problem): the various groups, especially the Djerbans and the Gabèsans, within the Tzidkat Hayim congregation can thereby express their devotion and adherence to a single house of worship; [6] the symbol itself has become enriched and extended, thereby eliminating a source of friction between the two groups of congregants who adhere to it.

The Commemoration of Two Gallant Men

In Judaism it is customary to commemorate the deceased on the anniversary of his death as well as on certain other occasions. During the morning synagogue services a prayer is recited wherein the deceased is mentioned by name. In the Sephardi rite to which southern Tunisians adhere, the prayer formula for rabbis and for laymen is not the same. That for rabbis is more florid; in it reference is made to the wisdom, learning, and outstanding piety of the deceased. These are qualities that are greatly esteemed in traditional Judaism, particularly in southern Tunisian Jewish tradition. In southern Tunisian Jewish sentiment there is also the feeling that great rabbis are endowed with supernatural powers, and

[6] Peters (1960), discussing the dynamics of genealogies in an analytical context comparable to mine, has used the term "area of ambiguity." See also the application of the concept in an analysis of village politics (Shokeid [Minkovitz] 1967a), and its development by Marx (1967:192–193). I feel that viewing in a single frame of discussion such phenomena as rabbinical innovations on the one hand and manipulations of Bedouin genealogies on the other within "areas of ambiguity" might be very fruitful and revealing of the varieties of sociocultural mechanism.

local folklore is full of stories of miracles that happened because of them (Noy 1968). Rabbis are conceived of as wise, dispassionate, soft-spoken, reserved, but deliberate. When deceased rabbis are commemorated the whole congregation rises. The memorial prayer for laymen is shorter, lacking the florid introduction, and no one rises in honor of the deceased, with the possible exception of the closest relatives, such as sons and grandsons.[7]

Early in 1965, Ayara was struck by tragedy. Through the town runs a stream which flows only during the height of the rainy season (a *nahal*). At this time the riverbed is apt to fill within a few days with a swift treacherous current. It is common knowledge in the region that in midwinter it is practically impossible to retrieve anything or to save anyone from the current of this kind of stream and that one should keep one's distance from its banks during this short period of the year. A little girl accidentally fell into the stream one day during the winter of 1965. An immigrant, new in Israel and unaware of the dangers involved in this particular natural phenomenon, jumped in after the child in a hopeless attempt to save her. A young soldier witnessing the incident also tried to save the child. All three lost their lives. The tragedy of the accident caught the emotions of people throughout the town and the country.

The soldier, the little girl, and the other man were immigrants from Morocco. The father of the soldier was at the time a congregant of the Tzidkat Hayim synagogue, but his

[7] I hesitate on this point because the ritual takes place when a close relative stands next to the Torah scroll during the public reading. It is customary for the relative's junior next-of-kin to cluster around him to receive his blessing and kiss his hand. Thus the deceased's next-of-kin are likely not to be seated anyway.

son had never attended that synagogue. When a year had passed and it was time to commemorate the death of the soldier, Rebee Yosseif, who led the prayer service, honored his memory by deliberately and emphatically reading the prayer reserved for the great and the wise. In the prayer he mentioned not only the soldier, whose father was present, but also the other man. Practically none of the congregants, most of them Tunisians, had known either one, yet the memory of these two strangers of alien origin was granted a singular honor. There was not the slightest suggestion that these men had been either particularly pious or learned. Everyone was well aware that they had been quite ordinary people who perhaps did not even observe basic ritual. The congregants, however, had wished to acknowledge their selfless act of sacrifice, for the two men had in the congregants' opinion acted as paragons of selflessness and as exemplary citizens and Israelis. They had reacted instinctively to a situation of immediate danger to another person and had allowed themselves to be governed by compassion, disregarding their own persons and their families.

The commemorative text for eminent rabbis that Rebee Yosseif, the leader of the congregation, read on the anniversary of their death begins as follows:

But where shall wisdom be found?
And where is the place of understanding?   [Job 28:12]
Happy is the man who finds wisdom and
The man who gets understanding   [Proverbs 3:13]
How abundant is your goodness
Which you have laid up for those
Who fear you, and wrought for
Those who take refuge in you . . . !   [Psalms 31:20]

The deep respect felt by the congregants found expression in the revered hush in which the congregation commemorated these two men as though they had been the most eminent, wise, and pious of Tunisian rabbis. The congregants ignored the fact that the accident underlined only too tragically the lack of wisdom of the deceased, their temperamental characters, and their total subjugation to natural phenomena—qualities contradictory to those traditionally attributed to great Tunisian rabbis. Furthermore, normally only rabbinical personalities with whom the congregation is very familiar, either personally or through oral report within the congregation, are honored as rabbis. In the present instance the congregation granted this honor to alien persons of whom nothing was known beyond the bare account of their one act of sacrifice. The symbol of the memorial prayer was thus extended to honor socially insignificant persons whose station in life was low and to encompass virtues beyond the traditionally accepted ones.

The two incidents that follow concern symbolic changes made by two leaders of the congregation, Rebee Yosseif, who has been mentioned previously, and Rebee Shushan. I am interested in understanding the actions of these men phenomenologically; I am not concerned whether in these actions they represent their congregations or whether these are idiosyncrasies of individual persons. In fact I believe that one of the major tasks of the anthropologist of culture is to discover the existential logic of "idiosyncrasies." Culture generally is composed of the actions of individuals, and there are always points in the course of action of individuals where the normative dictates of culture are articulated ambiguously, if at all. The study of individual idiosyncrasies, in the sociocultural terms of the locale in which they are enacted, is therefore crucial to an anthropological understanding of that locale.

The Changing of High Holy Days Garments

Perfect Sage Rebee Yosseif is the most popular of the ritual circumcisers (*moheil*) in Ayara. He is invited to officiate in the homes of people of all ethnic categories. A happy sixty-year-old extrovert, he races through the town on his bicycle from one ceremony to the next, his silver beard flowing in the wind. Rebee Yosseif, who stems from a rabbinical family in Djerba, spent most of his life in southern Tunisia, except for a few years before immigrating to Israel, when he lived in the north. In the circumcision ceremonies that he performs in Ayara, Rebee Yosseif is remarkably receptive to varieties of customs. Basically, the circumcision ritual he performs is that of Djerba, but he has adopted some northern Tunisian variants of customs. These he practices gleefully, not only in the homes of northern Tunisians, but even in the homes of Djerbans. He has also adopted customs and melodies of ethnic groups completely strange to him, for example, Moroccan customs. On one occasion I observed that he chanted a Moroccan hymn in a Tripolitanian home. From long discussions with Rebee Yosseif on these matters, I gained the clear impression that he was motivated by a desire that his ceremonies be lively, aesthetic, and acceptable to everyone.

Rebee Yosseif's disposition to adapt to his new environment and circumstances expressed itself in a most remarkable act—he changed his first (given) name. Although this was not a religious act, I draw it into the discussion because it illuminates Rebee Yosseif's general social situation and facilitates the interpretation of the religious changes which he adopted so readily. Rebee Yosseif's original name had been a traditional Djerban Jewish name which in the Judeo-Arabic spoken by Moroccans has a sexually obscene connotation. Rebee Yosseif was sensitive enough to the culture and language of immigrants from Morocco to feel embarrassed at the name which he had had for nearly sixty years. In order to escape the embarrassment that he now felt, he officially changed his given name—a most unusual act in his environment.

One of Rebee Yosseif's striking religious changes is his attire in the synagogue on the High Holy Days. Abroad, it was customary to wear a special white garment on New Year and on the Day of Atonement, two major festivals in the Jewish calendar. Rebee Yosseif, like most other immigrants in Ayara, discarded this and other traditional garments soon after immigrating to Israel because, he explained to me, "people laugh at us." For several years after his immigration he wore a European-styled black suit on New Year; in 1966, however, he donned a white European-styled suit which he had especially made and which he wore on the festivals.

The varied customs that this one man adopted are indicative of a desire to commune with ethnically different people. Rebee Yosseif expressly wishes to be a well-liked circumciser, not only among the Djerbans but among all the inhabitants of Ayara, and so he is. Therefore he discarded the name that is "obscene" and the garments that are "ludicrous" in the eyes of people of a different ethnic group. On the other hand, however, Rebee Yosseif wants to continue to adhere to ancient religious symbols, namely wearing white garments on the High Holy Days, but in doing so he does not want to express an ethnic identity that he considers unfashionable and embarrassing. This he achieves by imaginatively innovating the symbol. He divorces that which the white symbolizes from its immediate association, the traditional garment which represents the life and culture of Jewish Djerba, and transfers it instead to what he conceives to be symbolic of the modern Israeli way of life. The color of the new garments continues to express conventional religious sentiments, (the precise nature of which need not concern us here). The interesting finding is that the new garments now also express Rebee Yosseif's experience of Israel's varied styles of life and culture. He thus innovated the ancient religious practice of white dress on the High Holy Days, making it consistent with his approach to life and people, his adjustment to the new environment, and his current social situation.

The Correction of Mistakes during Service

I turn to the activities of another leader of the congregation, Perfect Sage Rebee Shushan, the teacher of the daily class of religious studies held at the Tzidkat Hayim synagogue. A morose and touchy character, he prides himself on his proficiency in modern Hebrew and on his knowledge of the rudiments of French. And indeed his correct usage of Hebrew stands out in his social environment. Rebee Shushan is self-conscious about his lack of modern education, and he is convinced that were it not for this failing he would be much further up the social ladder. He is also convinced that had he immigrated to Israel in his youth, his present station in life would have been much higher socially and economically than it is. He never tires of telling about his abortive attempt to immigrate in his youth. Now, he feels that his life has been wasted. Moreover, though only in his late forties, Rebee Shushan is ailing. His eyesight was failing rapidly at the time of research, he was then already unable to read (some years later he became totally blind) and he taught his class without recourse to books. Relying on his excellent memory, he was able to instruct his pupils in the fine details of cantillation, which demands a thorough knowledge of the Hebrew texts.

There was a certain measure of competition between Rebee Shushan and the other two prominent religious figures of the congregation, one of whom was Rebee Yosseif. These two leaders publicly read the Torah in the synagogue, while the nearly-blind Rebee Shushan could not engage in this act of prestige because the ritual requires that the text actually be read and not recited orally.

At public Torah reading during religious services Rebee Shushan's behavior was unusual. He made a point of correcting the slightest mistake in pronunciation by the reader, interrupting the reading very frequently and at times delivering lengthy discourses on points of grammar in the middle. Such interruption of the Torah reading in the event of mistakes in pronunciation and in cantillation is legitimate and accepted, but Rebee Shushan very much exaggerated the practice. Furthermore, Rebee Shushan's comments and corrections often stemmed from his objections to some of the peculiarities of the Hebrew pronunciation of southern Tunisians.[8] He claimed that the reading was incorrect, formulating his opinions in terms of social values—the desirability of having a uniform Hebrew pronunciation— and that there ought to be "an Israeli formula" (*nussakh yis-raeli*) in prayer and in speech. He claimed that his northern Tunisian pronunciation was identical with the "Israeli" pronunciation, whereas that of southern Tunisia was a local variant that differed from the accepted, normal,

[8] I am not aware of any published studies on the language of southern Tunisian Jews, but for some relevant information see Cohen 1964; also Lachman 1940.

and everyday Israeli style. An objective evaluation of Rebee Shushan's linguistic objections is not in place here; [9] significant for our purpose is the fact that he chose to rationalize in this particular manner his unusual religious behavior.

What did Rebee Shushan achieve in taking this course of action? By continuously interrupting the men who were reading the Torah he staked his claim to part of the honor given to them. Through these acts of scholarly ingenuity, he sought to gain a prestige similar to that of the men whom he corrected and to come to terms with his oncoming blindness. He convinced himself and those around him that, though blind, he nevertheless excelled in a skill that necessitates keen eyesight; in this way, he demonstrated to himself and to others that he could overcome his infirmity. Through his rationalizations of the interruptions, Rebee Shushan sought to bridge the gap that he felt existed between himself and society at large. He sought to divest the reading of the texts of its ethnic particularities and to innovate it, to invest the Torah-reading act with a "modern" and "Israeli" content, that it might serve as an instrument to effect rapport with what Rebee Shushan conceived as general Israeli culture. The Torah reading act was consistent with Rebee Shushan's other personal problems, his sense of frustration at having, in his opinion, failed in life because of his belated immigration to Israel and his limited participation in what he conceived as modern and Israeli culture. Rebee Shushan's experience of heterogeneity together with his other personal circumstances

[9] The particular Hebrew pronunciation that is taught in Israeli schools and which is considered good speech is referred to as "the Sephardi pronunciation." Despite the name it is not identical with any traditional pronunciation of the language; it is a new hybrid that emerged in the last century (see Blanc 1968).

caused him to adopt a course of ritual action that implied enhancement and acceptance of the strange and wider general culture of Israel.

Significance of Symbolic Changes

In all the changes I have discussed, the worshipers give symbolic expression to their new situation, specifically to the social heterogeneity in that situation. This symbolic expression or act is a means through which the worshiper seeks communion with the people of alien ethnic background among whom he now lives and with the strange society with which he interacts. I trace this principle in the four instances of symbolic change that were described.

(1) The solution of the Djerbans' problem concerning the name of the synagogue (involving a contradiction between symbol and experience) is indicative of the mutual adaptation and integration of the two main social groups in the congregation. The theoretical possibility of solving the problem by a Djerban attempt to change the name of the synagogue would have caused a confrontation between the Djerbans and the Gabèsans and was, as far as I could gather, never considered.

(2) In the commemoration incident, the congregation evaluated the persons concerned according to new criteria—universal virtues—yet bestowed on them the honor invested in the symbol of commemoration whose original reference is the traditional criteria of scholarship and piety, which were ignored here. The fact that the congregation was not familiar with the men involved was also disregarded.

(3) Rebee Yosseif's adaptation of the ritual symbol of the white color to modern dress is essentially an attempt at bridging the gulf between the norms and styles of living that

prevail inside the synagogue and those prevailing outside it. It is an effort to align the synagogical style of living with the mundane Israeli style of living.

(4) Finally, Rebee Shushan's rationalizations for interrupting the Torah readings are also attempts at associating the traditional act of Torah reading with the culture that he conceives as new, fashionable, and Israeli. He seeks to dissociate the act from undertones that are specific to a particular ethnic subculture that he considers undesirable, in this case the Djerban subculture.

Common to all these changes in symbolism is the fact that together with the changes the actors also express their reaction to the experience of contact with strangers and to life in a heterogeneous society. The effect of these actions is to bring about a symbolic rapport with the wider Ayara society which is beyond the secluded ethnic and religious circle of the Tzidkat Hayim people. They are steps in the process of passing beyond the boundaries of ethnicity and tradition and forging identities as citizens and Israelis.

Until now I have viewed the symbolic changes from the substantive aspect. We have followed the content and meaning of the changing symbols in terms of the culture in which they are expressed. The changes can also be viewed in more analytical terms. Proceeding from the premise that religious symbolic action in general stands in a close relationship with the existential situation of the worshipers, it follows that symbolic changes consist analytically in a shift of the particular relationships that formerly obtained. The category of religious change that conceptualizes the foregoing data is that of "innovation." In our instances, the symbolic actions are infused with content from a range of experience that the worshipers had not known in the past: the ethnic and cultural heterogeneity of their new environment in Israel had been absent from their existential situations in the Diaspora. The new experiential content is infused into the traditional symbols and exists side by side with the old theological contents of the symbols. In our instances, (3) excepted, the traditional diffuse experiential content of the symbolic actions is the sensation of respect for the Torah and for the men whose lives exemplify it. In the naming of the synagogue (1), the ambiguity of the symbol is manipulated so that it might accommodate additional content that stems from the problem of social heterogeneity. In the memorial prayer (2), the particular formula used had traditionally been reserved for those who excelled in learning and piety and with whom one was familiar. In the Tzidkat Hayim synagogue the human and civic excellence exhibited by the men who lost their lives was now conceived as akin to ancient Jewish piety, and the range of application of the ancient prayer formula was changed accordingly. Similarly, in (4), Rebee Shushan's interruptions represent an effort to divorce a traditional symbolic action from its association, inter alia, with a particular ethnic culture, and instead associate it, inter alia, with what he conceives to be fashionable and "Israeli." I stress the fact that Rebee Shushan's action is "inter alia" because there is no reason to doubt that in his behavior he also wishes to express conventional religious sentiments. The only novelty in Rebee Shushan's behavior is the quantitative exaggeration of the interruptions, particularly the rationalization, which expresses the sensation of cultural heterogeneity and striving for citizenship.

Finally, in instance (3) Rebee Yosseif's white garments are also a symbolic response to the experience of cultural heterogeneity exactly like Rebee Shushan's innovation, the difference being that in this instance the traditional religious sentiment associated with whiteness leads us to traditional Jewish color symbolism and sentiments, and not directly to the sentiment of devotion to the Torah and its scholars. Setting this substantive difference aside, Rebee Yosseif, from an analytical point of view, is, like Rebee Shushan, engaged in an act of religious innovation. Through his adherence to the ancient symbol of white garments, he seeks to express conventional religious sentiment associated with color symbolism, and through the specific change from Djerban pantaloons to a white European suit, he expresses and seeks to resolve his experience of cultural heterogeneity. In all these instances the new experiential content infused into the symbolic action molds the action into a particular form and direction without excluding the old experiential content. It is this aspect of the changes that separates them analytically from other types of religious change that I discussed in the previous chapters.

CHAPTER 8

The Evolution of Kinship Ties among Moroccan Immigrants

MOSHE SHOKEID

Many sociologists and anthropologists have studied geographical and social mobility under modern conditions and the effect of this mobility on the structure of traditional family groups and networks, both in tribal and in industrialized societies. Some studies particularly focus on patterns of adjustment of mobile individuals and mobile nuclear families to new situations in which they are separated from their closely knit social networks (e.g., Hellman 1948, Mitchell 1956, Bott 1957, Young and Willmott 1957, Epstein 1961). The study of family change has indicated that the mobile person living, working, and spending his leisure time among strangers develops empathy for and commitments toward strangers and distant relatives, who become his "friends," and take the place of his previous institutionalized obligations toward strictly defined categories of consanguineously or affinally related persons. More important, however, the former sanctioned familial considerations and preferences are often out of tune with his new social experience.

Comparatively few studies have focused their analysis primarily on the patterns of relationships between the dispersed members and units of the previously closely knit social networks of relatives. Among those who have I refer in particular to Litwak (1960a, b), who showed the continuity of important social contacts and material exchange between kin in spite of geographical and social mobility in modern society (see also Firth *et al.* 1969).

I intend to emphasize the dual nature of the process of adjustment under the conditions of modern existence in a complex society: on the one hand, adjustment to the new environmental and social counterfamilial demands, and on the other hand, the integration of the old familial expectations and obligations into the new pattern of existence. In considering this dual adjustment, I intend to deal with the latter aspect, namely, how people adjusting to new normative expectations perceive their previous obligations, and how they behave when confronted with demands made by members from their previous closely knit networks of relatives. This confrontation and the pressures it provokes may be instrumental, moral, emotional, or all together.

The fieldwork for this study was also carried out in Romema. In Morocco the Romemites had lived in Amran, part of a closely knit community. The other residents of Amran, including close kin and affines of the present Romemites, had settled in various other Israeli villages and towns. Thus the former Amranites were not only dispersed in Israel, but were also subject to incentives and pressures of new economic pursuits and opportunities. At a gathering (which I shall later describe in detail) between a few Romemites and a group of their relatives, former residents of Amran settled in an Israeli village distant from Romema, I witnessed a confrontation between past and present conditions of existence and a confrontation between the conflicting expectations of various relatives. The following description and analysis of the behavior of the former Amranites illustrates some of the features of the dual adjustment referred to above. I particularly stress those elements in the confrontation that lead to conflict between the present reality and the previous set of values and obligations obtaining among relatives.

The Separation and Meeting of Relations

The whole population of Amran migrated to Israel in 1956. On their way the Amranites had contemplated settling together in one village. They could not conceive of the possibility of being dispersed and settled in different places. Their wishes coincided with the policy of the settlement authorities [1] at that time (many difficulties had arisen in villages populated by immigrants from different countries, so established in line with an earlier policy derived from the melting pot theory).[2] Thus in the late 1950s, the policy was to found, as much as possible, homogeneous communities. In this way they hoped to ensure social stability in the newly established villages.[3] To the satisfaction of both the settlement authorities and the newcomers, all the former Amranites were immediately settled in Yashuv, a village in the north of the country. The village (houses and farms) had been planned, however, for a population of sixty nuclear families, while the Amranites were eventually registered as comprising seventy-five. The authorities suggested that the extra fifteen families be settled in an adjacent village, approximately two kms. from Yashuv. But the Amranites refused to

[1] See the Introduction.

[2] A policy resulting from the aspirations for a united society. This policy led to the establishment of heterogeneous rural communities composed of people from different countries, continents, and different cultural backgrounds.

[3] For the policy of establishing homogeneous communities see Minkovitz (now Shokeid) 1967b.

separate and the extra families shared accommodation with their closest relatives. Only after a few months did some of the families who lived under particularly crowded conditions agree to leave for the adjacent village.

The rapid economic and social changes and pressures caused severe strains, and bitter quarrels soon broke out among the Amranites. About a year after settlement these led to the dramatic decision of thirty-three families to leave the rest of their relatives, neighbors, and countrymen for another village, Romema, in the south of the country, about 150 kms. from Yashuv (see Shokeid 1971b:41, 43), a considerable distance in a country as small as Israel. A few more families gradually left Yashuv for other villages and towns. At the time of my research (October 1965–March 1967), only thirteen families of the former Amranites were left in Yashuv. The houses and farms which had been left vacant by the departing Amranites have since been settled by immigrants from other parts of Morocco and from eastern Europe.

In Morocco the Amranites consisted of seven patronymic groups, each identified by its separate family name (Sebag, Mahluf, Biton, Eluz, Gabay, Ben-Hamu, and Amzlag), but interrelated by marital ties. The migrants to Romema consisted mainly of members of the Sebag, the Biton, and the Mahluf groups (at the beginning almost equal in number) and a few members of the Amzlag family. The Amranites who remained in Yashuv were mainly of the Mahluf family with a few members of the Sebag and Amzlag families. The Sebags in Romema (as well as the few Sebags in Yashuv) were closely related by many affinal ties to the Mahluf families in Yashuv.

Since the split in 1957, the Amranites in Romema and

Yashuv, closely related by ties of kinship, affinity, and past friendship, have been reconciled. Mutual visits, marked by elaborate preparations and celebrations, take place. Some months after my arrival in Romema, I was approached by a few Romemites who planned to go to Yashuv, asking me to take them for a one-day trip by car. The main reason for the Romemites' trip was to visit Joshua Mahluf, leader of the Amranites in Yashuv, who had recently recovered from an arm injury. Initially, nine persons planned to go either in my car or with a hired van. By the eve of the departure only five were able to leave the next morning for Yashuv. The other four had withdrawn mainly because some urgent work had to be done on their farms (such as spraying and weeding). It was therefore decided that three members of the company would go with me and the other two by public transport. The latter left for Yashuv the next morning at 6:30 A.M., while we left at 8:00 A.M. The traveling party consisted of three Sebags, a Mahluf, and a Biton, three of whom were members of the village committee. Though it was by chance that the three main family groups which dominated the internal politics of Romema were represented among the travelers, this fact might have had some relevance to the later events. The Sebag travelers were: Zevulun, in his late fifties, a member of the Sebag senior generation; Shlomo, in his early forties (a nephew of Zevulun), a successful farmer and a member of the village committee who was a shrewd politician; Nahum, in his late twenties, a nephew of Zevulun and a cousin of Shlomo, a fairly successful farmer liked by all. The other two travelers were Reuben Mahluf, in his early thirties, who was successful in his economic enterprises and was a member of the committee; and Noah Biton, in his early thirties, a popular figure in Romema and the chairman of the village committee. Although Noah Biton was the only one of the five who had no clear kinship or affinal ties with the people of Yashuv, he was nevertheless, together with Shlomo Sebag, one of the more prominent guests, who all together formed a distinguished group of visitors.

Joshua, whom the Romemites wanted to visit, was agnatically related to Reuben Mahluf, and closely related to the Sebags by affinal ties. His mother was a sister to Zevulun's mother who was grandmother of Shlomo and Nahum. He and his brother were married to Sebag women and his sister was the widow of Zevulun's deceased brother (see Figure 1).

We took along a sack of large cones of sugar to be distributed as gifts to people in Yashuv. At noon we arrived at Joshua's house in Yashuv; the Romemites who had gone by bus arrived soon afterward. Joshua and his family made us welcome and immediately offered us tea and almonds. While

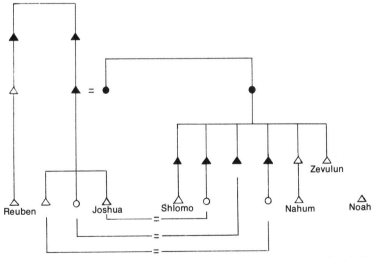

Figure 1. Consanguineal and affinal ties between Joshua Mahluf and his Romema guests

lunch was being prepared, some Yashuv women, formerly from Amran, came to greet us. The lunch, a lavish affair, including dishes of chicken, mutton, vegetables, fruit, and various alcoholic and soft drinks, was soon served. During lunch Joshua gave us a detailed description of his injury. Soon after lunch, a local relative of Joshua took one of Joshua's sheep to be slaughtered in the adjacent village where a qualified slaughterer was available; the sheep was to be served for dinner. In the meantime, we went with Joshua to look at his farm. On returning from the fields, Joshua and Shlomo prepared the slaughtered sheep for cooking while the rest of us sat around chatting. It was already late afternoon, and the guests were planning visits to a few more Yashuv families. Shlomo and Noah were drawing up a schedule of visits (or a "plan of visits" as they told me) for the rest of their stay. But Joshua interfered, declaring that since they were his guests he would not let them go anywhere else. This firm claim was followed by noisy but humorous arguments in which a few of the Yashuv women took part. It was eventually agreed that Joshua would go with his guests for a visit to one of the local Amzlag families.

Early in the afternoon a close friend of Joshua, who was of Tunisian origin and a settler in a nearby village, had joined us. He seemed to be highly respected by his Moroccan neighbors and took full part in all the events of that day and evening. We all went to the home of the Amzlags where we had tea and fried chicken. Here we met a settler of Moroccan origin who was not related to the Amranites by kinship or by affinal ties but had settled in Yashuv after the 1957 split of the Amranites. After a short visit at the Amzlags, all present left for Joshua's house, where a sumptuous dinner was served. At the table were seated the five guests from Ro-

mema; Joshua and his brother; two Amzlags, son and grand-
son of Joshua and Zevulun's uncle (their mothers' brother);
Joshua's nephew Moshe Sebag; and David and Ezra Sebag,
brothers, residents of Yashuv and affinally related to Joshua.
The three local Sebags were nephews of Zevulun and
cousins of Shlomo and Nahum from Romema (Figure 2
shows the kinship ties between the Yashuv hosts and the
Romema guests). Apart from the former Amranites four
"strangers" were present: the Tunisian, two local Moroccans,
and the anthropologist. Altogether, sixteen men attended
the festive meal.

The table was heavily laden with alcoholic and soft drinks.
The first course was chicken, followed by two helpings of

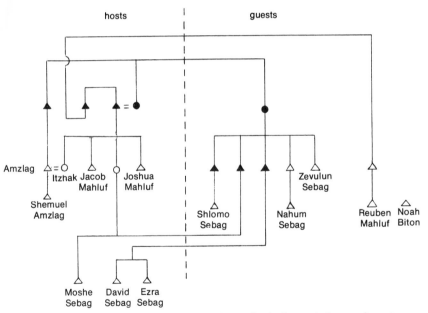

Figure 2. Kinship ties between Yashuv hosts (including only former Amranites) and Romema guests

mutton from the sheep which had been slaughtered earlier. Joshua was serving his guests and encouraging them to eat and drink as much as possible. One of the local unrelated Moroccans entertained and indeed delighted the company with stories and jokes about the adventures of Moroccan immigrants in Israel. We had already drunk four bottles of brandy and one bottle of arak (an oriental alcoholic drink) when a fierce argument arose between the storyteller and Shlomo Sebag from Romema, who was seated next to him. The argument was about Shlomo's drinking habits. The storyteller blamed him for drinking less than the others and thus for being unfair. Shlomo and the "Moroccan" were consequently watching each other's drinks carefully and demanding that the others drink as much as they did. The frequency of giving toasts was quickly increasing while the storyteller and the other unrelated Moroccan were watching the way the guests from Romema took drinks, in order, as they said, to maintain justice.

We had already had seven bottles of alcohol when the two local Sebag brothers (David and Ezra) started another noisy argument. They suddenly began to criticize sharply the manner in which the Romemites had visited Yashuv. They complained that except for Joshua no settler in Yashuv had been informed of the Romemites' intention to visit Yashuv. Shlomo and Noah argued, however, that they had sent a letter to Joshua telling him that they intended to visit him and the rest of "his family." (They thus included in the term "his family" all the Amranites in Yashuv.) Joshua intervened in support of the local Sebags; he argued that he did not behave like the Romemites—namely, coming to Romema for such "ridiculously" short visits. He went on to tell how last year he had persuaded David and Ezra to join him on a visit to

Romema for a circumcision and a *bar-mitzvah* in Zevulun's family in Romema, although the brothers had not at first been particularly keen to go. Amidst ever increasing noise to the point of bedlam, Nahum shouted that he was going to stay in Yashuv till Sunday. Joshua, heedless of the din, went on to relate that he had had to cut short his last visit to Romema because of an unpleasant incident ("the point"— *nekudah*—as he called it) which had taken place on the Sabbath he was there. Here he stopped without further comment on the unfortunate "point." One of the local unrelated Moroccans however spoke gravely of despicable "secrets" (*sodot*) concerning the Sabbath in Romema. At that point, Shlomo Sebag, extremely agitated, jumped up from his seat and in a voice charged with emotion said that his heart was "burning" with the pain caused to him by the realization that after a year since Joshua's visit to Romema he still did not know about the "secrets" which Joshua was telling to "strangers" (*zarim*). The atmosphere was highly charged: Romema guests and Yashuv hosts were shouting at one another and seemed ready at any moment to express their hostility in physical terms. The main dispute, however, was between Shlomo Sebag and his Yashuv cousins, David and Ezra Sebag. Amidst the shouting it suddenly became clear to the Romemites through a comment by one of the unrelated Moroccans, that the "secret" mentioned earlier concerned an incident which had been known to the Romemites. The reference was to the refusal of one of the settlers of Romema to let Joshua read the *maftir* (a part of the synagogue prayer service) [4] on the Sabbath he was in Romema, which happened

---

[4] *Maftir*, whose literal meaning is "one who concludes," is the term applied to the three or more concluding verses of the weekly Torah portion read on the Sabbath, festivals, and public fast days. The person called up

to be the anniversary of the death of his father. The breach of hospitality and apparent disrespect to an honored guest was made by Barukh Mahluf (not related by any close family ties to Joshua or to his guests from Romema), because the same Sabbath was also the anniversary of his own father's death. As a resident of Romema, Barukh was entitled to that right; his refusal to give up that right during Joshua's visit appeared to the guests from Yashuv to show arrogance and lack of goodwill on the part of the Romemites as a whole.

Now that the nature of Joshua's grudge was out in the open, Shlomo stood up to tell the truth (as he claimed) and to give all the facts related to the sad incident—from its very beginning to the grave echoes in present life in Romema. In sharp contrast to the chaotic atmosphere which had previously dominated the gathering, a tense silence prevailed, due to Shlomo's impressive style of narrative as well as to the disciplinary measures imposed by Joshua's Tunisian friend, who firmly stated that anyone who disturbed Shlomo's narrative would immediately be forced to drink up a whole bottle of brandy. Shlomo said that he himself had vainly pleaded with Barukh in Romema to let Joshua read the *maftir*. The offense to a distinguished guest had, however, led to a decision by a majority of the congregants that no one in Romema would receive, under any circumstances, an honored part in ritual unless he paid for it (the Romemites referred to the custom as "the selling of *mitzvot*" [5]). A few weeks later, during an important festival, that decision caused a serious dispute in Romema. A Romemite refused to comply with the new ruling and was therefore not allowed to

---

to read these passages is called *maftir* as well. He also reads the *haftarah*, a portion from the Prophets read after the reading from the Torah.

[5] See Chapter 2 for further explanation of this custom.

officiate at the ritual, although it was the anniversary of his father's death. The incident led eventually to a split in the congregation and to the establishment of the Bitons' synagogue in Romema (see Chapter 2).

Although most of the details mentioned by Shlomo did happen at one time or another in Romema, it was nevertheless a farfetched story. Shlomo selected, arranged, and interpreted the facts to suit his personal message to the Yashuv hosts. He even called me as witness to confirm the story, although I had not been in Romema when the incidents had occurred. In fact, the split of the congregation in Romema was the end product of continued and extended internal disputes and rivalries in various spheres of life between the different groups of relatives in Romema (see Chapter 2). The last main dispute which finally led to the split was however related (as Shlomo Sebag had stated) to the refusal of a Romemite (a Biton, on the anniversary of his father's death), to pay for an honorific part during ritual. The dispute occurred a few months after Joshua's visit to Romema. I could not establish the authenticity of Shlomo's claim about the ruling which demands payments for honorific parts during ritual "under any circumstances" being connected with Joshua's visit. In any event, Barukh Mahluf, who refused to let Joshua have the discussed honor, was one of the most generous contributors to the synagogue's funds. At the same time, the disputes about "the selling of *mitzvot*" were part of a broader conflict in Romema which found particular expression in the sphere of ritual. The authenticity of Shlomo's story in which he proclaimed the Romemites' deep concern for their relatives and hosts in Yashuv, however, was not challenged. For the sake of the guests' relatives in Yashuv, Shlomo, in his story, sacrificed no less than the unity of Romema.

It was already 3:00 A.M. when dessert was served. Leaving Joshua's house, the company (Romemites and hosts) gathered in the front yard, and the question was again raised as to how the Romemites should spend the rest of their stay in Yashuv. Noah and Shlomo suggested that they continue visiting throughout the night. But the local Sebags, supported by some more persons from Yashuv, strongly resented the plan which they claimed was only a device to get the visits over with as quickly as possible and thus prevent complaints from the people of Yashuv. David Sebag from Yashuv argued that he could not eat any more and asked me to look at his hard and bursting belly.

The local Sebags were very offended and concluded that if the Romemites insisted on following their plan of a series of quick visits they might as well return immediately, for they in Yashuv could not care less. I was however called aside by the people of Yashuv who tried to find out if I could stay for another day. In a dilemma as to what to say, I told the truth. I said that I had all the time I wanted at my disposal to please myself but that the Romemites were unfortunately committed to return home before noon that day because of their various pressing responsibilities as watchmen, farmers, and so forth. My interrogators now loudly accused the Romemites of deliberately refusing to stay longer while using me as an excuse. It appeared that one of the Romemites had stated earlier that they had promised me to return home the next morning. In the midst of the discussion Nahum Sebag decided to go to bed and left together with one of his cousins, Moshe Sebag, Joshua's nephew. With their departure the disputants calmed down. The other Romemites went off eventually to visit Joshua's brother who took us to his home. We were joined by Ezra Sebag. At that late hour of the night, Joshua's brother awakened his wife and daughter, who immediately began to prepare tea and a proper meal. The guests, drowsy and heavy with food and drink, could hardly lift their heads to look at the many bottles of drinks and dishes of chicken and mutton. Three of them were actually asleep in their seats. After some efforts they were awakened and they mechanically tasted the food. It was past 4:00 A.M. when we finished that sleepy meal and went to bed.

At 6:30 A.M. we were already up and at morning prayers. After breakfast (which included boiled eggs, fish, chicken, fruit, and coffee) we visited the local rabbi, a cousin of Joshua, who had not attended last night's celebrations because he was in mourning for his brother, who had died a few months earlier. We did not expect to find him at home, since he had left the village early in the morning for the neighboring town where he was employed as a slaughterer. His wife nevertheless had kept careful watch since early morning to make sure that we would visit them. The rabbi's younger brother was on hand to entertain us. The guests tried to leave after tea, which was served with nuts, but their hostess insisted on feeding them a proper meal. Soft and alcoholic drinks were brought in and a dish of chicken was served. The guests ate very little and only Shlomo was finally obliged to drink some alcohol. The rabbi's wife wanted to serve other dishes, but her plans were foiled with the Grace after Meals prayer which was quickly begun. Soon afterward we left in spite of her protests.

Arriving at the center of the village (where my car was parked), the Romemites planned to go to the nearby village to visit an Amzlag family, but were met by Moshe Sebag, who complained that they had promised the night before to visit him that morning, at 7:00 A.M. The Romemites gave in and followed him to his house (where Nahum Sebag was staying). Coffee was soon served and a relaxed atmosphere prevailed. Some time after our arrival at Moshe's house, Joshua joined us. Moshe, however, was frequently reminded by the guests to tell his wife to hurry up with the meal, which included the same rich menu offered to us at the homes of Joshua and his brother the day before. In the meantime the Amzlag relative from the adjacent village had arrived and joined the table. This was the longest visit of that morning, and the Romemites even ate a little here. After leaving Moshe Sebag's home, they went to David Sebag's, accompanied by Moshe Sebag, their last host, as well as by Joshua and the Amzlag man from the nearby village. At David Sebag's home, the previous night's argument started all over again. The host bitterly complained that the Romemites rarely visited Yashuv, but worse, when they did come, their visits were offendingly short. He dramatically went on to tell about the frustration he had suffered at the celebration of the birth of his youngest daughter. He complained that he had sent out invitations in good time to his relatives, most of whom were in Romema. On the day of the celebration David Sebag and his guests waited until quite late for his relatives from Romema, who never came. The celebration finally started without them. The Yashuv rabbi was blessing the guests, referring separately to the host, his family, and his guests, and he went on to bless also the host's relatives in Romema. But David said that at this point he intervened with the rabbi, raised his glass, and declared: "To hell (*lazazel*) with my relatives in Romema." David then explained his extreme annoyance at the celebration, which he did not mind expressing vociferously: "I am alone in Yashuv and my relatives neglect me as if I were an orphan. When my cousin in Naham [a village in the south of the country] invited me to attend his wedding, I left on Tuesday [the day of the wedding] although I had to begin next day to irrigate my fields of peanuts. I could not leave my cousin alone!! When I came back to Yashuv on the following Sunday [after attending the wedding itself and the celebrations that followed] [6] I went immediately to look at the fields of peanuts. The crop was all burned [dried up]!! The same happened a few years before when I attended Naftali Sebag's wedding in Romema. I realized that another cousin of mine in Romema, Hanan Sebag, was going to get married within a few days. I went home to tell my wife and returned immediately to Romema. When a kinsman invites you to a celebration nothing in the world should be an obstacle which can stop you from coming; let the fields be burned!!" [7]

David's complaint, however, did not stop Reuben Mahluf and Zevulun Sebag from leaving at 11:00 A.M. by bus for Romema as they had planned. The rest of the Romemites stayed a while, trying to do justice to the food (which included fish, chicken, mutton, and so forth) and drinks. David

[6] According to my observations the main celebrations at Moroccan weddings take place between the eve of the wedding and the following Sabbath.

[7] During my fieldwork I witnessed wedding ceremonies in Naham (the village mentioned by David Sebag) and observed the behavior of the guests from Romema who were expected to stay until the Sabbath (according to religious precepts Sabbath traveling is forbidden). At the wedding in question eventually most of the female guests stayed while most of the men stayed only the night of the wedding (which happened to be on a Wednesday) and the following morning. They returned to Naham on Friday afternoon and stayed for the Sabbath. I should mention that Romema and Naham are in the same region and traveling between them was not too difficult.

sighed in despair at the Romemites' complete inability to tackle the food. Joshua, Moshe, and the Amzlag visitor were eating well. The arguments about the Romemites' manner of visiting in Yashuv started again. Joshua suggested that the Romemites stay till evening and then he would go with them to Romema. The Romemites in their turn suggested that they would return with me to Yashuv for a long visit in the near future during which they would stay for a full day with every family of relatives in Yashuv. Joshua was sceptical. Shlomo defended himself by an unfortunate spontaneous defense, pleading that he must go home to irrigate his recently planted fields of sugar beet, to which Joshua reacted mercilessly with the statement: "The man who runs after Mammon, Mammon escapes him." Shlomo was offended, and addressing me he protested: "Everybody thinks that we people of Romema are rich." I felt obliged to react to Shlomo's protest and said that it was better to be thought to be wealthy than to suffer poverty. Thereafter the atmosphere became cheerful and all present agreed that there were in Romema only four unfortunate poor families and one miserable settler who in spite of his great wealth lived in poverty.

Keeping up relationships with their relatives provided the Romemites with an apparently objective and indeed meaningful yardstick to measure their economic and social success in Israel. Since the departure of the Romemites from Yashuv they were constantly comparing their achievements and failures with those of the Amranites who had remained in Yashuv (see Shokeid 1971b:47). This observation is generally true for the dispersed Amranites anywhere in Israel, who constantly measured their achievements with those of their relatives elsewhere. This comparison seems to be objective and valid, since on their arrival in Israel they had all had the same opportunities and were confronted with the same difficulties. I think that close relatives anywhere form an important and permanent yardstick with which to measure one's success in life, due to the notion, true or false, that relatives possess similar intrinsic potentialities.

We were preparing to leave. The Romemites were already seated in my car, obviously relieved. Our hosts filled whatever space was left in the car with bags of peanuts, their main harvest of the season. Moshe and David Sebag, the latter no longer agitated, goodheartedly reminded Nahum of the declaration he had made yesterday evening that he would stay in Yashuv till Sunday. Greetings and happy cheers accompanied our departure. It was almost noon when we left and we arrived in Romema late in the afternoon.

Ceremonial Intensity versus
the Loosening of Kinship Bonds

In Morocco the Romemites had hardly ever been confronted with the problem of spending time with their relatives. Most of them lived together in the small community of Amran, and therefore could meet one another constantly; neither the peddlers nor the traveling craftsmen remained away from Amran for any length of time. They used to leave for a few days or weeks and then return home for a time. Rarely had they to face the dilemma of whether or not to miss an important engagement, economic or social, for the sake of participating in a relative's wedding or visiting a sick relative. Usually they could, with little effort, accommodate family business to economic and other pursuits. They used to visit one another regularly on the Sabbath and the festivals, as is still the custom among the residents of Romema and Yashuv.

The 150-kilometer distance between Romema and Yashuv involves a long and difficult journey since there is no direct route by public transport between Romema and Yashuv. When not going by private car, the Romemites had to transfer to four different buses in order to get to Yashuv. Moreover, those buses frequently stopped on the way to pick up passengers and were often very crowded. Traveling to Yashuv was, therefore, a very tedious journey, taking about half a day one way. Thus the former Amranites, living now in Romema and Yashuv, could no longer see one another regularly.

The distance and the discomfort of travel were not the only obstacles to the former Amranites coming together as often as they had wished; another obstacle was the new type of occupation they had taken up. Apart from the geographic dispersion, immigration to Israel led to a change in occupation whereby the former peddlers and craftsmen of Amran became farmers. In Morocco the working schedule had been much more flexible, given to personal manipulation, and there had been periods during the winter in which the Amranites did not travel at all, but stayed at home. Mixed farming in Israel, on the other hand, created a continuous and very rigid schedule. The Romemites could not delay, even for a few days, such tasks as planting, irrigating, weeding, spraying, picking, and sorting, without causing serious damage to their crops. Since they usually had a variety of crops, a flock of poultry, and herds of sheep, they were bound to their farms all year round. Moreover, most of the Romemites had additional occupations as guards and tractor drivers. Their additional employment gave them even less freedom of movement and kept them to an even more rigid schedule which did not allow them to absent themselves for any length of time from Romema.

Under the constraints exercised upon the Romemites in their new environment, the bonds of former compulsive obligations toward their kin were loosened. Their paramount concern, now, was to adjust to their new way of life and new economic framework and undertakings, even if this meant neglecting their relatives. The Romemites entered a new phase in the division of labor in society in which they could shift and extend their loyalties, obligations, and resources to new and numerous associations and pursuits. Their involvement could now be, in the main, only in simplex relationships, depending upon the wishes and the investments, whether emotional, material, or otherwise, of the participants in these relationships.

The details of the Romemites' trip and their behavior during the visit in Yashuv show, however, that they tried at the same time to continue their intimate relationship with their kin. But the nature of their familial relationships remained absorbing and demanding, calling for all-embracing loyalties from its participants. The Romemites, who continued to visit their relatives, had at each visit to cope with strong demands, particularly those concerning allocation of time to their relatives. While they were unable to fulfill those demands, the Romemites did not challenge their moral validity. They became involved in a conflict of obligations or in a moral debt which they would not be able to settle in any foreseeable future. The previous, greatly intermeshed, severely sanctioned reactions toward the claims of kin were replaced by conscious dilemmas and the obvious making of choices which were followed by increased anxiety in the relationships between relatives. David Sebag of Yashuv, who emphatically declared that "there is nothing in the world which should be an obstacle to stop you from coming to a kinsman's celebration, let the fields be burned!" was challenging the Romemites' order of priorities in which kinship ties were not primary. In this he was expressing the opinion and feelings of many others in Yashuv.

I have omitted from this discussion the analysis of the roles played by certain participants; [8] however, it is possible that

[8] Although I focused my analysis on the general problem of the loosening of kinship ties, attention should be given to individual behavior, motives, and roles which greatly influence the event. Those who figured particularly in the case were David Sebag, Shlomo Sebag, Joshua, and the "strangers." On this occasion the Sebags in Yashuv were very much offended by the changing patterns of relationships between relatives: although three among the guests were Sebags, priority in visits went to others rather than their close kinsmen. They first visited Joshua Mahluf, then an Amzlag family, Joshua's brother, and only after that the Sebags. In fact, the Romemites had almost to be forced to visit their Sebag relatives in Yashuv. The Romemites' choice of visits must therefore have been a painful matter to the Yashuv Sebags, in particular to David and his brother Ezra. Moshe Sebag was in a more comfortable position, since he was the favorite nephew of Joshua. In the role of spokesman David Sebag emphasized the Romemites' shortcoming as a whole in the sphere of behavior toward relatives. Joshua, who acted as chief host, though he refrained from becoming intensively involved, nevertheless exerted great influence in the disputation. Shlomo Sebag had the main role among the guests, probably because he was the best spokesman of the Sebags, who were mainly under attack, and because he was one of the influential leaders of Romema. Zevulun Sebag was removed from the direct quarrel mainly because he represented the older generation and therefore deserved respect from a gathering most of whom were his nephews. Nahum Sebag, both in age and social position, was the junior among the guests. A most important role was played by the "strangers," particularly by the unrelated Moroccans who first opened the series of quarrels and discussions. The latter, well acquainted with Moroccan traditions as well as with the internal relationships of the Amranites, brought to the fore the moral dilemmas con-

the behavior of the people of Yashuv was influenced by the presence of three members of the village committee of Romema who also represented its three family groups and therefore represented Romema as a whole. That observation implies that the profound complaint of the people of Yashuv about the breach of general principles of behavior between relatives was rooted in the nature of the confrontation, which was with a communal delegation rather than with individual persons.

In Amran, as in many other Middle Eastern societies, the sharing of food, particularly meat provided from the host's herd, is symbolic of friendly relationships. The host's act expresses his respect toward his guests, and the offering and partaking of the food is a manifestation of mutual commitment between host and guest.[9] Thus it was only natural for Joshua to slaughter a sheep for his guests from Romema. The other hosts in Yashuv also insisted on serving the Romemites meat.[10] It should be noted that the sharing of food with

---

cerning relationships between relatives and had apparently been the provokers in the subsequent quarrel. They thus spared the hosts from committing a possible breach of courtesy by being disagreeable to their guests, but helped to bring the grievances out in the open. The other "strangers" present, the Tunisian and the anthropologist, representing different ethnic traditions, were instrumental in moderating the quarrel. The Tunisian, who was allowed to keep in check the participants' overt behavior, reassured them that the manifestations of mutual hostility would not get out of hand. The anthropologist by his silence confirmed Shlomo's myth, which greatly influenced the resolution of conflict. See for example Frankenberg's analysis (1957) of the role of "stranger" and "outsider" in a Welsh village.

[9] For further description and analysis of the exchange of visits between kinsmen see Marx 1967:164–171.

[10] The symbolic meaning of sharing meat remained potent among the Amranites even if the meat was not of an animal taken from the host's herd and even if the animal was not slaughtered in honor of the guests.

guests (whether relatives or not), a custom perpetuated from Morocco, was as important and compulsive in Romema as it was in Yashuv. My observations in Romema led me to the conclusion that a guest's refusal to accept the food offered was tantamount to refusing to establish close social relationships. Thus, for example, some instructors (usually veteran Israelis either of European or Middle Eastern origin) who did not like Moroccan food or hesitated to eat the Romemites' food because of hygienic or ritual considerations were unintentionally emphasizing the cultural and social differences between them and the Romemites.[11]

To visit their relatives in Yashuv in a manner that would conform with the propriety customary in Amran called for a visit of at least three days. Such a period would have allowed them to visit quite leisurely, and do justice to the food and drinks offered to them in a potlatch manner at most of the homes of the thirteen families in Yashuv. The Romemites, however, could rarely afford a vacation of three successive days without encountering severe difficulties both with their farming and with other pursuits.[12] Visiting Yashuv for only

[11] The Romemites constantly insisted that I share their food and invited me for meals on the Sabbath and on festivals way in advance; they also invited me for meals on other occasions. At table, they insisted that I specifically eat meat and particularly drink liquor as much as possible. As an ecstatic mood developed during those meals, nourished by the delicious food and the intoxicating drinks, the Romemites, through affectionate remarks, such as "we are like brothers," expressed our intimate relationship.

[12] I have indicated elsewhere (see, e.g., Chapter 4) that settlement in the *moshav* was followed by the dissolution of the traditional extended household unit. The Romemites, who farmed extensively and also had additional occupations apart from farming, could therefore rarely (or only under conditions of emergency) commit themselves to help others, including their own brothers.

one day, on the other hand, caused much frustration to guests and hosts alike. The visitors could not stay with only one family in Yashuv without offending their other local relatives. Yet to attempt to visit properly most of the Yashuv families in one day would have been a vain effort. The guests simply could not consume the huge quantities of food and drinks offered to them on the many quick successive visits they had to make in that short time, and therefore could not do justice to the main expression and symbol of close relationships.

In their history till the split in 1957, Romema guests and Yashuv hosts could recall many quarrels and struggles about various personal, economic, social, political, moral, and daily issues. They were now, bitterly quarreling about the amount of time spent and the food consumed by the Romemites as guests. Thus the gathering of kinsmen, planned as a joyful and ceremonial event, turned into turmoil. The disorder reflected the confusion the former Amranites sensed in the field of norms and priorities which command social relationships.[13] That pathetic scene in which guests appeared to be discourteously and rather aggressively treated,[14] while generous hospitality seemed to be offensively ignored, was in fact a struggle over the very essence of the bond relationships between the two parties. It was as if through the massive intake of food offered, regardless of physical limitations, mu-

[13] That event recalls Geertz's observations (1957) of the breakdown of a funeral ritual caused by the confusion of values, which also occurred in a situation of changing environmental, social, and cultural conditions.

[14] The antagonistic behavior expressed toward the guests during the gathering at night could, however, be later forgiven on the excuse of excessive drinking of alcohol. See, for example, Szwed's analysis (1966) on the functions of alcohol consumption at meetings.

tual relationships between guests and hosts as close relatives would prove to be intact, in spite of the eroding process of estrangement caused by environmental and social conditions prevailing since immigration to Israel. I proffer here the hypothesis, which demands further investigation, that the importance of the sharing of food as a symbol of close relationships has increased in Israel, where other instrumental ties have weakened and where mutual dependence between the former Amranites has decreased. While actual meetings between relatives have decreased, the symbolic significance of the ceremonial and the ritual which are performed at the meeting of relatives have augmented. The pains—physical and emotional—experienced both by guests and hosts, the dramatic reconciliation during the gathering at night, the reopening of the dispute and its final reconciliation during the next day, all these made the visit a success in terms of its significance for the participants. The reception of the Romemites was not a polite entertainment of guests according to traditional norms of hospitality as still practiced both in Romema and Yashuv, but a stormy and feverish event to be long remembered and talked about in both communities. Thus, the short time the Romemites spent in Yashuv waxed with the catharsis the participants went through during the ceremonial of reunion.

We have, throughout this book, described and analyzed the ways in which North African immigrants in Israel coped with the existential problems and dilemmas of their new environment in the personal, social, and cultural spheres. The case of our concluding chapter—the feverish reunion of the former residents of a closely knit Atlas Mountains community—encapsulates the immigrants' trials of social passage, the vigorousness of their response to the bewilderments of social existence in Israel, as well as the ways they have come to terms with its inevitabilities.

Bibliography

Abihassera, Y. 1967. *Aleif Binah*. Yavne: Keren Lehoza'at Sefarim. In Hebrew.

Allouche, F. 1928. "Vision tunisienne," *La Revue littéraire juive* 2:69–71.

Ames. M. 1963. "Ideological and Social Change in Ceylon," *Human Organization* 22:45–53.

Apter, D. E. 1963. "Political Religion in the New Nations." In *Old Societies and New States*, edited by C. Geertz. New York: Free Press. Pp. 57–104.

Arditti, R. 1904. "Un rabbin tunisien du XVIIè siècle: R. Hai Taib," *Revue tunisienne* 11:489–494.

Baldwin, E. 1972. *Differentiation and Co-operation in an Israeli Veteran Moshav*. Manchester: Manchester University Press.

Barnes, J. A. 1967. "Some Ethical Problems in Modern Fieldwork." In *Anthropologists in the Field*, edited by D. G. Jongmans and P. C. W. Gutkind. Assen: Van Gorcum. Pp. 193–213.

Baxter, P. T. W. n.d. "Fieldwork in Three African Societies: The Boran of North Kenya, The Bakiga of South-West Uganda and Some Ghanaian Villages." University of Manchester, manuscript.

Beidelman, T. O. 1970. "Some Sociological Implications of Culture." In *Theoretical Sociology: Perspectives and Developments*, edited by J. C. McKinney and E. A. Tiryakian. New York: Appleton-Century-Crofts. Pp. 499–523.

Bellah, R. N. 1964. "Religious Evolution," *American Sociological Review* 24:358–374.

Ben-David, J., ed. 1964. *Agricultural Planning and Village Planning in Israel*. Paris: UNESCO.

Bensimon-Donath, D. 1968. *Evolution du judaïsme, marocain sous le Protectoret français*. Paris: Mouton.

Berger, P. L. 1958. "Sectarianism and Religious Sociation," *American Journal of Sociology* 64:41–44.

Blanc, H. 1968. "The Israeli *Koine* as an Emergent National Standard." In *Language Problems of Developing Nations*, edited by J. A. Fishman, C. A. Ferguson and J. Das Gupta. New York: Wiley. Pp. 237–251.

238   Bibliography

Boissevain, J. B. 1969. *Saints and Fireworks: Religion and Politics in Rural Malta*. London: Athlone, University of London.

Bott, E. 1957. *Family and Social Network*. London: Tavistock.

Bredmeier, H. C. 1955. "The Methodology of Functionalism." *American Sociological Review* 20:173–180.

Busia, K. 1966. *Urban Churches in Britain*. Lutterworth.

Chaudhri, J. 1969. "A Typical Support Structure of Leadership in Punjab: The Faction." University of Manchester, unpublished thesis.

Chouraqui, A. 1972. *La Saga des Juifs en Afrique du Nord*. Paris: Hachette.

Cohen, A. 1965. *Arab Border Villages in Israel*. Manchester: Manchester University Press.

——. 1969. *Custom and Politics in Urban Africa*. London: Routledge & Kegan Paul.

Cohen, D. 1964. *Le Parler arabe des Juifs de Tunis*. Paris: Mouton.

Colson, E. 1953. *The Makah Indians*. Manchester: Manchester University Press.

——. 1971. *The Social Consequences of Resettlement: The Impact of the Kariba Resettlement upon the Gwembe Tonga*. Manchester: Manchester University Press.

Cooke, J. D. 1927. "Euhemerism: A Mediaeval Interpretation of Classical Paganism," *Speculum* 2:396–410.

Davis, K. 1948. *Human Society*. New York: Macmillan.

Deshen, S. 1965. "A Case of Breakdown of Modernization in an Israeli Immigrant Community," *Jewish Journal of Sociology* 7:63–91. Rev. version in *Integration and Development in Israel*, edited by S. N. Eisenstadt *et al.* Jerusalem: Israel Universities Press, 1970. Pp. 556–586.

——. 1966. "Conflict and Social Change: The Case of an Israeli Village," *Sociologia Ruralis* 6:31–55.

——. 1969a. "The Ethnic Synagogue: A Pattern of Religious Change in Israel." In *The Integration of Immigrants from Different Countries of Origin in Israel*, edited by S. N. Eisenstadt. Jerusalem: Magnes Press. Pp. 66–73. In Hebrew.

——. 1969b. "Non-Conformists in an Israeli Immigrant Community," *Mankind Quarterly* 9:166–177.

——. 1970. *Immigrant Voters in Israel: Parties and Congregations in a Local Election Campaign*. Manchester: Manchester University Press.

Douglas, M. 1966. *Purity and Danger: An Analysis of Concepts of Pollution and Taboo*. London: Routledge & Kegan Paul.

Dumont, L. 1970. *Homo Hierarchicus: The Caste System and its Implications*. London: Weidenfeld & Nicholson.

Eisenstadt, S. N. 1953. *The Absorption of Immigrants*. London: Routledge & Kegan Paul.

——. 1967. *Israeli Society: Background, Development and Problems*. London: Weidenfeld & Nicholson.

——. ed. 1969a. *The Integration of Immigrants from Different Countries of Origin in Israel*. Jerusalem: Magnes Press.

——. 1969b. "Some Observations on the Dynamics of Traditions," *Comparative Studies in Society and History* 11:451–475.

——. 1973a. "Post Traditional Societies and the Continuity and Reconstruction of Tradition," *Daedalus*, Winter.

——. 1973b. *Tradition, Change and Modernity*. New York: Wiley.

Elkin, F. 1969. "Advertising Themes and Quiet Revolutions: Dilemmas in French Canada," *American Journal of Sociology* 75:112–122.

Epstein, A. L. 1961. "The Network and Urban Social Organization," *Rhodes-Livingstone Journal* 29:29–62. Also in *Social Networks in Urban Situations*, edited by J. C. Mitchell. Manchester: Manchester University Press, 1969.

Evans-Pritchard, E. E. 1949. *The Sanusi of Cyrenaica*. Oxford: Clarendon Press.

Fél, E., and T. Hofer. 1972. *CA* Book review of *Proper Peasants*. *Current Anthropology* 13:479–497.

Firth, R. 1936. *We, the Tikopia*. London: Allen & Unwin.

Firth, R., and J. Spillius. 1963. *A Study in Ritual Modification: The Work of the Gods in Tikopia in 1929 and 1952*. Royal Anthropological Institute Occasional Paper No. 19. London.

Firth, R., et al. 1969. *Families and Their Relatives*. London: Routledge & Kegan Paul.

Flamand, P. n.d. *Les Communautés israélites du Sud-Marocain: Essai de description et d'analyse de la vie juive en milieu berbere*. Casablanca: Imprimeries Réunies.

Fortes, M. 1967. *The Web of Kinship among the Tallensi*. London: Oxford University Press. First published 1949.

Frankenberg, R. 1957. *Village on the Border*. London: Cohen & West.

——. 1963. Participant Observers. *New Society* 1, 22:22–23.

Frazier, E. F. 1964. *The Negro Church in America*. Liverpool: Liverpool University Press.

Ganzfried, D. 1961. *Code of Jewish Law*. New York: Hebrew Publishing Co.

Geertz, C. 1957. "Ritual and Social Change: A Javanese Example," *American Anthropologist* 59:32–54.

——. 1960. *The Religion of Java*. Glencoe, Ill.: Free Press.

——. 1962. "Social Change and Economic Modernization in Two Indonesian Towns." In *On the Theory of Social Change*, edited by E. E. Hagen. Homewood, Ill.: Dorsey Press. Pp. 385–407.

——. 1964. " 'Internal Conversion' in Contemporary Bali." In *Malayan and Indonesian Studies: Essays Presented to Sir Richard Winstedt*, edited by J. Bastin and R. Roolvink. Oxford: Clarendon Press. Pp. 282–302.

——. 1966. "Religion as a Cultural System." In *Anthropological Approaches to the Study of Religion*, edited by M. Banton. Association of Social Anthropologists Monograph No. 3. London: Tavistock. Pp. 1–46.

Gluckman, M. 1955. *The Judicial Process among the Barotse of Northern Rhodesia*. Manchester: Manchester University Press.

——. 1962. "Les Rites de passage." In Gluckman, ed., *Essays on the Ritual of Social Relations*. Manchester: Manchester University Press. Pp. 1–52.

——. 1965. *Politics, Law and Ritual in Tribal Society*. Oxford: Blackwell.

Goody, J. 1969. "Adoption in Cross-Cultural Perspective," *Comparative Studies in Society and History* 11:55–78.

Haviv, Y. 1966. *Never Despair: Seven Folktales related by Aliza Amidjar from Tangiers*. Haifa: Ethnological Museum and Folklore Archives, Israel Folktale Archives, Publication series No. 13. In Hebrew, Preface in English.

Hellmann, E. 1948. *Rooiyard: A Sociological Survey of an Urban Native Slum Yard*. Rhodes-Livingstone Paper No. 13. Cape Town: Oxford University Press.

Herberg, W. 1960. *Protestant, Catholic, Jew*. New York: Doubleday.

Hirschberg, H. Z. 1965. *A History of the Jews in North Africa*. Jerusalem: Bialik Institute. In Hebrew.

Hofer, T. 1968 "Anthropologists and Native Ethnographers in Central Europe: Comparative Notes on the Professional Personality of Two Disciplines," *Current Anthropology* 9:311–315.

Homans, G. C., and D. M. Schneider. 1955. *Marriage, Authority and Final Causes*. Glencoe, Ill.: Free Press.

Huri, H. 1971. "Sermon in Memory of Rebee Nissim Haddad," *Or Tora* 4:122–132. In Hebrew.

Jacobs, M. 1956. *A Study of Cultural Stability and Change: The Moroccan Jewess*. Washington: Catholic University of America Press.

Johnson, R. 1957. "A Critical Appraisal of the Church-Sect Typology," *American Sociological Review* 22:88–92.

——. 1963. "On Church and Sect," *American Sociological Review* 28:539–549.

Karo, J. 1960. *Orah Hayim*. Jerusalem: Pe'er Ha'Torah. In Hebrew. 1st ed., Venice, 1565.

Katz, J. 1960. "Traditional Society and Modern Society," *Megamot* 10:304–311. In Hebrew, English summary.

——. 1961. *Tradition and Crisis: Jewish Society at the End of the Middle Ages*. Glencoe, Ill.: Free Press.

Köbben, A. J. F. 1967. "Participation and Quantification: Fieldwork among the Djuka." In *Anthropologists in the Field*, edited by P. C. W. Gutkind. Assen: Van Gorcum. Pp. 35–55.

Kuper, H. 1970. *A Witch in My Heart*. London: Oxford University Press.

Lachmann, R. 1940. *Jewish Cantillation and Song in the Isle of Djerba*. Jerusalem: Archives of Oriental Music, The Hebrew University.

Leach, E. R. 1963. Book Review of *Caste in Modern India and Other Essays* by M. N. Srinivas, 1962, Bombay, Asia Publishing House, *British Journal of Sociology* 14:377–378.

Lévi-Strauss, C. 1966a. "The Scope of Anthropology," *Current Anthropology* 7:112–123.

——. 1966b. "Anthropology: Its Achievements and Future," *Current Anthropology* 7:124–127.

Litwak, E. 1960a. "Geographic Mobility and Extended Family Cohesion," *American Sociological Review* 25:385–394.

——. 1960b. "Occupational Mobility and Extended Family Cohesion," *American Sociological Review* 25:9–21.

Long, N. 1968. *Social Change and the Individual*. Manchester: Manchester University Press.

Malinowski, B. 1948. *Magic, Science and Religion*. Glencoe, Ill.: Free Press.

Maquet, J. J. 1964. "Objectivity in Anthropology," *Current Anthropology* 5:47–55.

Marriott, M. 1955. "Little Communities in an Indigenous Civilization." In *Village India: Studies in the Little Community*, edited by M. Marriott. Chicago: University of Chicago Press. Pp. 171–222.

Martin, D. A. 1965. "Towards Eliminating the Concept of Secularization." In *Penguin Survey of the Social Sciences*, edited by J. Gould. London: Penguin. Pp. 169–182.

Marx, E. 1967. *Bedouin of the Negev*. Manchester: Manchester University Press.

Matthes, J. 1962. "Bemerkungen zur Saekularisierungsthese in der neueren Religionssoziologie," *Koelner Zeitschrift fuer Soziologie und Sozialpsychologie*, Sonderheft 6:65–77.

Maybury-Lewis, D. 1965. *The Savage and the Innocent*. London: Evans.

Minkovitz, *see* Shokeid, M.

Mitchell, J. C. 1956. *The Kalela Dance.* Manchester: Manchester University Press.

Niebuhr, H. R. 1929. *The Social Sources of Denominationalism.* New York: Holt.

Noy, D. 1964. *Jewish Folktales from Morocco.* Jerusalem: Bitfuzot Hagolah. In Hebrew, Preface in English.

——. 1968. *Contes populaires racontés par des Juifs de Tunisie.* Jerusalem: World Zionist Organization.

Palgi, P. 1966. "Cultural Components of Immigrants' Adjustment." In *Migration, Mental Health and Community Service,* edited by H. P. David. Washington: International Research Institute.

Paul, B. D. 1953. "Interview Techniques and Field Relationships." In *Anthropology Today,* edited by A. L. Kroeber, *et al.* Chicago: The University of Chicago Press. Pp. 430–451.

Peel, J. D. Y. 1968. "Syncretism and Religious Change," *Comparative Studies in Society and History* 10:121–141.

Peters, E. L. 1960. "The Proliferation of Lineage Segments among the Bedouin of Cyrenaica," *Journal of the Royal Anthropological Institute* 90:29–53.

Peven, D. E. 1968. "The Use of Religious Revival Techniques to Indoctrinate Personnel: The Home-Party Sales Organization," *Sociological Quarterly* 9:97–106.

Pfautz, H. 1955. "The Sociology of Secularization: Religious Groups," *American Journal of Sociology* 61:121–128.

Poll, S. 1961. *The Hassidic Community of Williamsburg.* Glencoe, Ill.: Free Press.

Pope, L. 1942. *Millhands and Preachers.* New Haven: Yale University Press.

Radcliffe-Brown, A. R. 1952. "Taboo." In Radcliffe-Brown, ed., *Structure and Function in Primitive Society,* London: Cohen & West. Pp. 133–152.

Robertson, R. 1970. *The Sociological Interpretation of Religion.* Oxford: Blackwell.

Schechter, S. 1908. "Safed in the Sixteenth Century: A City of Legists and Mystics." In Schechter, ed., *Studies in Judaism.* Philadelphia: The Jewish Publication Society. Pp. 202–288. (Also in *The Jewish Expression,* edited by J. Goldin. New York: Bantam Books. Pp. 258–321.)

Scholem, G. G. 1955. *Major Trends in Jewish Mysticism.* London: Thames and Hudson. First published 1941.

——. 1965. "Tradition and New Creation in the Ritual of the Kabbalists." In Scholem, ed., *On the Kabbalah and Its Symbolism.* New York: Schocken. Pp. 118–157.

Seznec, J. 1953. *The Survival of the Pagan Gods: The Mythological Tradition and its Place in Renaissance Humanism and Art*. New York: Pantheon.

Shack, W. A. 1968. "The Masqal-Pole: Religious Conflict and Social Change in Gurageland," *Africa* 38:457–468.

Shapiro, O. 1971. *Rural Settlements of New Immigrants in Israel*. Rehovot: Settlement Study Center.

Shiner, L. 1967. "The Concept 'Secularization' in Empirical Research," *Journal for the Scientific Study of Religion* 6:207–220.

Shokeid (Minkovitz), M. 1967a. *From Lineage to Association: Family Organizations in the Process of Adjustment to the Moshav*. Jerusalem: Hebrew University. In Hebrew, English summary.

——. 1967b. "Old Conflicts in a New Environment: A Study of a Moroccan Atlas Mountains Community Transplanted to Israel," *Jewish Journal of Sociology* 9:191–208.

——. 1968. "Immigration and Factionalism: An Analysis of Factions in Rural Israeli Communities of Immigrants," *British Journal of Sociology* 19:385–406.

——. 1971a. "Social Networks and Innovation in the Division of Labour between Men and Women in the Family and in the Community: A Study of Moroccan Immigrants in Israel," *Canadian Review of Sociology and Anthropology* 8:1–17.

——. 1971b. *The Dual Heritage: Immigrants from the Atlas Mountains in an Israeli Village*. Manchester: Manchester University Press.

Singer, M. 1972. "Urbanization and Cultural Change: *Bhakti* in the City." In Singer, ed., *When a Great Tradition Modernizes*. London: Pall Mall Press, Pp. 148–196.

Spiro, M. E. 1966. "Religion: Problems of Definition and Explanation." In *Anthropological Approaches to the Study of Religion*, edited by M. Banton. Association of Social Anthropologists Monograph No. 3. London: Tavistock. Pp. 85–126.

Srinivas, M. N. 1952. *Religion and Society among the Coorgs of South India*. Oxford: Clarendon Press.

——. 1966. *Social Change in Modern India*. Berkeley: University of California Press.

Szwed, J. F. 1966. "Gossip, Drinking, and Social Control: Consensus and Communication in a Newfoundland Parish," *Ethnology* 5:434–441.

Tavuchis, N. 1963. *Pastors and Immigrants: The Role of a Religious Elite in the Absorption of Norwegian Immigrants*. The Hague: Nijhoff.

Tiryakian, E. A. 1970. "Structural Sociology." In *Theoretical Sociology*, edited by J. C. McKinney and E. A. Tiryakian. New York: Appleton-Century-Crofts. Pp. 115–137.

Tishby, I. 1960. *The Doctrine of Evil and the Kelippa in Lurianic Kabala.* Jerusalem: Schocken Library. In Hebrew.

Troeltsch, E. 1931. *The Social Teaching of the Christian Churches.* London: Allen & Unwin. First published 1912.

Turner, V. W. 1957. *Schism and Continuity in an African Society.* Manchester: Manchester University Press.

———. 1960. "Muchona the Hornet, Interpreter of Religion." In *In the Company of Man,* edited by J. B. Casagrande. New York: Harper. Pp. 333–355.

———. 1966. "Ritual Aspects of Conflict Control in African Micro-politics." In *Political Anthropology,* edited by M. J. Swartz, V. W. Turner, and A. Tuden. Chicago: Aldine. Pp. 239–246.

———. 1967. *The Forest of Symbols.* Ithaca: Cornell University Press.

———. 1968. *The Drums of Affliction.* London: Oxford University Press.

Van Velsen, J. 1967. "The Extended-Case Method and Situational Analysis." In *The Craft of Social Anthropology,* edited by A. L. Epstein, London: Tavistock. Pp. 129–149.

Vidich, A. J. 1955. "Participant Observation and the Collection of Data," *American Journal of Sociology* 60:354–360.

Waal Malefijt, A. de. 1968. *Religion and Culture: An Introduction to Anthropology of Religion.* New York: Macmillan.

Weingrod, A. 1966. *Reluctant Pioneers: Village Development in Israel.* Ithaca: Cornell University Press.

Weintraub, D. 1971. *Immigration and Social Change: Agricultural Settlements of New Immigrants in Israel.* Manchester: Manchester University Press.

Weintraub, D., M. Lissak, and Y. Atzmon. 1969. *Moshava, Kibbutz and Moshav: Patterns of Jewish Rural Settlement and Development in Palestine.* Ithaca and London: Cornell University Press.

West, J. 1945. *Plainville U.S.A.* New York: Columbia University Press.

Westermarck, E. 1926. *Ritual and Belief in Morocco.* London: Macmillan.

Wyllie, R. W. 1968. "Ritual and Social Change: A Ghanaian Example," *American Anthropologist* 70:21–33.

Whyte, W. F. 1964. *Street Corner Society.* Chicago: University of Chicago Press. First published 1943.

Willis, R. G. 1968. "Changes in Mystical Concepts and Practice among the Fipa," *Ethnology* 7:139–157.

Willner, D. 1969. *Nation-building and Community in Israel.* Princeton, N.J.: Princeton University Press.

Wilson, B. 1966. *Religion in Secular Society.* London: Watts.

Yinger, J. M. 1963. "Religion and Society: Problems of Integration and

Pluralism among the Privileged," *Review of Religious Research* 4. Also in *The Sociology of Religion: An Anthology*, edited by R. D. Knudten. New York: Appleton-Century-Crofts, 1967. Pp. 496–512.

Young, M., and P. Willmott. 1957. *Family and Kinship in East London.* London: Routledge & Kegan Paul.

Zborowski, M., and E. Herzog. 1964. *Life Is with People: The Culture of the Shtetl.* New York: Schocken. First published 1952.

Zenner, W. 1965. "Memorialism: Some Jewish Examples," *American Anthropologist* 67:481–483.

Index

THE PREDICAMENT
OF HOMECOMING

Designed by R. E. Rosenbaum.
Composed by Vail-Ballou Press, Inc.,
in 11 point linofilm Janson, 3 points leaded,
with display lines in Helvetica.
Printed offset by Vail-Ballou Press
on Warren's No. 66 text, 50 pound basis,
with the Cornell University Press watermark.
Bound by Vail-Ballou Press
in Columbia book cloth
and stamped in All Purpose foil.

65